FASTING AS A WAY OF LIFE

Fasting has been a way of life, voluntarily or involuntarily, since primordial man first began to scrounge for food and to try to placate an avenging divine power.

Modern man foregoes food principally to lose weight the quickest and easiest way; to give the body a rest; to feel better physically and mentally; and to save money on food bills. But there are more than a score of other reasons to fast.

The applications of fasting are proliferating in our busy, stressful, consciousness-expanding, health-seeking society. Employees of an enlightened manufacturer in the Midwest fast for a sense of renewal. Star athletes train on "the ultimate diet." Hundreds of thousands of Americans—from every walk of life—altruistically celebrate the Thursday before Thanksgiving as a national fast day.

—From the Author's Note

Bantam Books by Allan Cott, M.D., with Jerome Agel
and Eugene Boe

FASTING: THE ULTIMATE DIET
FASTING AS A WAY OF LIFE

Fasting
as a Way of Life

by Allan Cott, M.D.

with Jerome Agel
and Eugene Boe

produced by Jerome Agel

BANTAM BOOKS
TORONTO · NEW YORK · LONDON · SYDNEY

FASTING AS A WAY OF LIFE
A Bantam Book / May 1977
2nd printing . . . . January 1978
3rd printing . . . . July 1979
4th printing . . . . . . August 1980
5th printing . . . . December 1981

ISBN 0-553-20856-X

Published simultaneously in the United States and Canada

Bantam Books are published by Bantam Books, Inc. Its trade-
mark, consisting of the words "Bantam Books" and the por-
trayal of a rooster, is Registered in U.S. Patent and Trademark
Office and in other countries. Marca Registrada. Bantam
Books, Inc., 666 Fifth Avenue, New York, New York 10103.

PRINTED IN THE UNITED STATES OF AMERICA

14 13 12 11 10 9 8 7 6

Note

Fasting has been a way of life, voluntarily or involuntarily, since primordial man first began to scrounge for food and to try to placate an avenging divine power.

Modern man foregoes food principally to lose weight the quickest and easiest way; to give the body a rest; to feel better physically and mentally; and to save money on food bills. But there are more than a score of other reasons to fast.

Because nature takes good care of the body during a fast, the person in average good health can fast safely for up to four weeks. (A long fast should be done only under the direct supervision of a doctor experienced in the fasting procedure.)

The applications of fasting are proliferating in our busy, stressful, consciousness-expanding, health-seeking society. Employees of an enlightened manufacturer in the Midwest fast for "a sense of renewal." Star athletes train on "the ultimate diet." Hundreds of thousands of Americans—from every walk of life—altruistically celebrate the Thursday before Thanksgiving as a national fast day.

Numerous applications of fasting are reported here, as are healthier eating regimens and medical-research discoveries. There is now reason to believe that the fasted body will not "accept" in quantity alcohol, nicotine, drugs, or other toxic substances.

People planning to fast on their own should find this book informative and supportive. But *Fasting as a Way of Life* is not intended to take the place of professional care or consultation. As we strongly emphasized in *Fasting: The Ultimate Diet,* a person planning

to fast even for a day should—as with any diet—first
consult her or his doctor. Anyone undertaking a longer
fast should be under the doctor's close supervision
throughout the fast and for the entire period of adjust-
ment after the fast. Though fasting can be therapeutic,
the emphasis in this book is principally on fasting as a
way of life for people in at least average good health.

—*Allan Cott, M.D.*

Contents

Fasting
as a Way of Life

1.

Fear of Fasting

"I feel like a wisp of cloud, full of light and energy. It's a magical rest for my whole system."

"I've never felt so well, I've never been so thin, I've never had so much free time."

"I now have greater respect for my body's intelligence and capability. Fasting is a marvelous life-lesson."

"Once I got rid of the cultural hang-up that I've got to eat all the time, fasting was a snap!"

These are typical expressions reflecting the ease, comfort, and even exhilaration of the fasting experience.

Yet fasting remains controversial. There are still those whose attitudes toward going without food for even one day are frozen in fear and ignorance. "It's too dangerous," they say. Or "I'd pass out if I didn't eat 'three squares' a day." Or "I'm afraid I'd starve to death."

An ironic consequence of the popularity of my first book, *Fasting: The Ultimate Diet,* was that it revived some of those fears and prejudices, though I was confident my extensive documentation demonstrated them to be unfounded.

Incredibly, some doctors still believe it is "dangerous" for anyone to abstain from a single meal, and they resurrect the fallacies when asked about "the ultimate diet." Man is the only "animal" who persists in eating or is forced to eat even when he is sick, though he may have no appetite and food makes him nauseous.

~ (To some Americans, fasting may be idiosyncratic precisely because we are an overabundant society producing more foodstuffs than we need to consume.)

If disparaging doctors would take the time to examine the evidence dispassionately, they would finally stop warning of "dangers" that simply do not exist for most people. They owe it to their patients to become more knowledgeable because this remarkable discipline has stood the test of time—at least five thousand years.

It apparently needs to be said over and over again: "Fasting is *not* starving, fasting is *not* starving, fasting is *not* starving. . . ."

The body has in reserve at least *a month's* supply of food. It nourishes itself during a fast as if it were continuing to receive food. When this stockpile is consumed, the body signals by the return of appetite that it is time to start the refeeding program.

Dr. George F. Cahill, Jr., of the Harvard School of Medicine, put this crucial fact in a nutshell: "Man's *survival* is predicated upon a remarkable ability to conserve the relatively limited body protein stores while utilizing fat as the primary energy-producing food."

I know many grossly overweight people who still think of fasting as starving. They shy away from the idea of even a brief fast, even though they would benefit most from "the ultimate diet."

I remind these people that in many controlled experiments here and abroad it has been documented that the obese tolerate fasting far better than any other weight-reducing regimen. Such men and women find they can go long periods without feeling hungry, for the fasting body *automatically* dims the memory of food and normalizes metabolism. The rate of weight loss is also extremely supportive of self-esteem, which had diminished with each prior unsuccessful dieting experience.

(The food editor of a metropolitan newspaper, by her own admission, weighed 60 pounds more than she should. But she believed she couldn't consider fasting for even a day because she'd "starve to death." Also, she had been told by her doctor that anyone who fasts must be "insane.")

The body does not consume itself in any vital way even during an extended fast. This is the principal difference between the life-enhancing act of fasting and the self-destructive act of starving. But misleading books about fasting are still being published; they use the word fasting to describe a *starving* situation. Written possibly in ignorance, these books are grossly inaccurate and unfair to the reader, for they discourage fasting, especially the total fast. Even more reprehensible is the fact that many doctors still do not differentiate between fasting and starving.

When I explain the groundlessness of fears about *fasting,* I encounter the classic underlying inhibitions: "But won't I feel hungry and keep having hunger pangs?" "Won't I be faint and weak and have to stay in bed?"

My response to these concerns is based on tens of thousands of observed fasting experiences.

You will not be hungry. Any so-called hunger "pangs" are simply normal gastric contractions or stomach spasms. They represent the *sensation* of hunger rather than *true* hunger. Much of what we think of as hunger is really the desire for sensual nourishment and for pleasure and for warmth and for affection and for relief from boredom, frustration or loneliness.

To a very large extent, "hunger" is a conditioned reflex. ("If it's noon, I must be hungry and therefore I must eat.")

False appetite and stomach rumblings in the first few days are fleeting. They can be immediately quieted with a glass of water. (You should drink a minimum of two quarts of water every day of the fast.)

You will not feel weak or faint. In fact, you may discover new reservoirs of strength and vitality.

The very act of eating can be exhausting; it takes a lot of energy to digest food. When the body is freed from that chore, it naturally feels lighter and much more vibrant.

Not even during a lengthy fast should you stay in bed. As a matter of fact, the more activity, the better—within reason, of course. Exercise expedites the fasting process. It works as an appetite depressant by slowing the flow of insulin.

For decades the magazine *Physical Culture* reminded its readers that "fasting is an excellent agent for purifying the blood, and the majority of people who fast usually experience an increase in their ability to think more clearly. The five special senses of seeing, hearing, tasting, touching, and smelling become more acute during a fast."

As a psychiatrist, I am more than commonly aware of how attitude shapes the texture of any experience. What we expect in a situation is what we usually experience. If we approach something with an irrational dread, our unconscious may contrive to bring about adverse effects. As a colleague has wisely observed, you are practicing medicine on yourself every day as far as your own personal health is concerned.

There is simply no reason to be afraid of fasting.

Fasting is a revitalizing, reconstructive way of life which is healthful and inspirational. It is an adventure; it enriches body and soul. It is also, in the words of *Time* magazine, "the oldest, surest and quickest way to get rid of excess fat."

2.

Revitalization

Vogue magazine described fasting as "the newest and the most ancient practice. A religious rite. A historic mode of cleansing. A conditioner for meditation. A tool for consciousness-raising, for demonstration and protest."

Fasting can be defined in two words: *No eating.*

Purely speaking, it is the total abstention from caloric intake. It is a "diet" consisting only of water.

The definition of this discipline which surely is as old as man has become muddied in contemporary usage. One hears people say they're going on "a fruit juice fast" or "a vegetable juice fast" or "a bread-and-water fast." Some people say they're fasting when they eat a skimpy meal. A prominent California politician said he was "fasting by necessity—not choice" with a lunch of orange juice and a granola bar on the run. I have even read medical reports of fasts lasting 80 to 100 days—or longer. This is not possible! During a fast, appetite leaves on the fourth or fifth day. If the fast is not ended arbitrarily, appetite returns by the twenty-fifth to thirty-second day. When one continues to abstain from food after appetite returns, he is no longer fasting—he is starving!

The pure (water only) fast is a regimen which confers multiple benefits. To quote the second-century Greek physician Athenaeus, it "cures diseases, dries up bodily humors, puts demons to flight, gets rid of impure thoughts, makes the mind clearer and the heart purer, the body sanctified, and raises man to the throne of God." One of my colleagues has observed that fasting "hurriedly stops the intake of decomposition toxins. It gives the organism a chance to catch up with its work of excretion. It helps remove the toxins in the tissues. It causes the body to consume its excess of fat."

One of fasting's most alluring attractions—if not its *most* popular—is the dramatic loss of weight it accomplishes. It is "the ultimate diet" because weight is lost so much more quickly and easily than by any other weight-reduction method.

People who have a problem with weight basically have a problem with eating. Diets restricting the intake of certain foods or those top-heavy with other foods repeatedly fail because they do nothing to alter attitudes about food and eating. One can gain a new perspective on food and one's relationship to it by making fasting part of one's way of life—by fasting at regular intervals, preferably one day each week or three consecutive days in each month.

It is the somewhat overweight—but decidedly *not* obese—individual who feels most motivated to fast. He or she has gained weight and has enough self-esteem to want to look, feel, and actually *be* his or her best. (The "typical" faster is definitely not the compulsive overeater with deep-seated psychological disturbances. Such a person probably needs professional counseling and a thorough biochemical examination.)

Fasting improves personal appearance. The net result of weight loss is always a trimmer, more youthful appearance. The skin has a better color and texture after a fast. The eyes become clearer.

Fasting is a rejuvenating process; it can turn back the clock. Television's *Phyllis*—Cloris Leachman—likes to spread the word that fasting is a solution to the problems of the body. "It's simply wonderful. It can do practically anything. It is a miracle cure. It cured my asthma."

Miss Leachman thinks of all the water she drinks while fasting as "the fountain of youth." The minimum of at least two quarts a day serves a three-fold purpose:

(1) it prevents dehydration; (2) it stifles feelings of hunger; (3) it supplies minerals.

Drink the water even if you're not thirsty. Man can live a long time by water alone—but not by air alone.

Any kind of water whose chemical identification reads H_2O is fine. It should be at room temperature. I recommend bottled water, if it is available, rather than tap water. Most tap water contains chlorine and fluorides, manufactured chemicals. At a time when you are trying to cleanse your system, you should not be ingesting more chemicals. During a fast, many people find the taste and odor of tap water offensive.

I am sometimes asked if the water drinking doesn't add weight. It doesn't. When you eat nothing, the water you drink will be eliminated. The principal organ of elimination of water is not the kidneys but the skin with its millions of pores.

Alcoholic beverages must be avoided. Alcohol is highly caloric; during a fast, it can also be gravely injurious. This restriction can also serve as an obligatory start for anybody seriously wanting to resolve a drinking problem.

The longer the fast, the greater the chance the taste and yearning for alcohol will diminish. We have discovered that as the body and the palate purify themselves, they begin instinctively to reject the very *idea* of harmful substances.

It has been gratifying to see how many problem drinkers have been helped by a fast of even one week. Patients whom I would describe as heavy drinkers but not alcoholics routinely find their pattern of drinking modified. One prominent journalist told me her fast of only a week had helped her cut down from at least six drinks a day to two drinks—and often to none.

Fasting can also help break the self-destructive habit of smoking. I have had a number of patients who were able to give up smoking after a fast of only five or six days. None reported withdrawal symptoms or any desire to return to smoking. Fasting succeeded where all the New Year's resolutions—and other efforts—to stop smoking had failed.

The director of a weight-control camp in upstate New York is a remarkable example of someone who became an ex-smoker through fasting. She had smoked for thirty-seven years before going on two four-day fasts separated only by one day of light eating. She has not touched a cigarette since.

One of my patients told me how *her* fast had succeeded in "curing" even her boyfriend's addiction. On their first date after she had fasted and broken her smoking habit, she backed off from his kisses. "My God, the way your mouth smells!" she exclaimed. "I can't kiss you. It would be like kissing an ashtray." It was a variant of the old ultimatum "The lips that touch liquor must never touch mine!" Happily, her boyfriend made the right—and healthy—choice, deciding that kisses are better than nicotine.

A spectacular anti-smoking success story is related by Dr. Agatha Thrash of Yuchi Pines Health Institute in Seale, Alabama. She claims that 3,000 people—every participant in the program—have been "cured" permanently of their smoking habit through a five-day regimen. It begins with a day of total fasting, then a day of modified fasting (juices). On the third day, bread is added to the diet; on the fourth, vegetables; on the fifth, nuts. The regular diet is resumed on the sixth day. Dr. Thrash, a Seventh-Day Adventist, is convinced "a day or two of fasting—quickly clearing the body of nicotine and other toxins—will do most people more good than any amount of medical advice or treatment."

Not all people who fast have made such a clean and total break with a smoking habit, but most report they are smoking less—and enjoying it less.

We now have evidence fasting can be an effective modality for breaking the drug habit. The tranquility of a longer fast seems to obviate the need to return to artificial "highs" and escapes through "tripping."

Fasting can be a boon for insomniacs. Usually kept

awake by tension and anxiety, many find they are finally sleeping well. During a two-week fast, one of my correspondents reported, "I have been able to sleep through the night—every night—for the first time since I was a child." On the other hand, I have heard of fasters who find their energy level so elevated they cannot get to sleep. I advise anyone having trouble sleeping to exercise more than usual; exercise is a natural tranquilizer. A fast should replace tranquilizers, antidepressants, pep pills and barbiturates, anyway.

Reactions after a longer fast have included: ". . . tunes you in with the gentle voice of nature"; "I noticed a heightening of ethical and spiritual awareness. . ."; ". . . incredible euphoria"; and ". . . the occasion for a profound and insightful inner journey. . ."; it's like a month's vacation in the mountains or at the seashore."

3.

Getting Into It

You have decided to improve your life by fasting for a day or two or longer. You have rid your mind of all the false notions. You have your doctor's go-ahead. You are thoroughly familiar with the manifold benefits of the experience and you know millions of other people are doing it at this very moment.

But still you hesitate. You keep putting off "the day." You tell yourself you'll start tomorrow. Or next week.

How to translate good intentions into action? How to break through the procrastination?

There are ways of "psyching" yourself up.

If you are completely new to fasting, try skipping a meal or two on the day preceding the fast. This will give you a "taste" of discovering how easily you can get along without eating.

I tell all those fasting under my supervision that the first day or two may be trying but they will soon be quite comfortable.

First you must ignore the nay-sayers, who are always with us . . . the ones who are forever predicting something won't work or will have dire results. Negative feedback often comes from well-meaning friends and members of the family. Bear in mind you are doing something perfectly safe—something you chose to do, something that will benefit you, something *you can stop any time you wish.*

My colleague in Moscow, Dr. Yuri Nicolayev, who has supervised tens of thousands of long fasts, told me his fasting unit has a two- to three-year waiting list because former patients enthusiastically extol the experience and results.

Fasting is popular because it is easy and because it works!

It is not possible to describe definitively the fasting experience, any more than one can describe the feeling of parachuting or hang-gliding. As Kafka put it, "Just try to explain to anyone the art of fasting! Anyone who has no feeling for it cannot be made to understand it." Reactions indeed vary over the entire spectrum of human response. An individual may feel different from one day to the next, but mostly he will feel good. "Even a one-day fast informs the body it can sacrifice food in good stride," notes Joan Gussow, chairman of the program in nutrition at Columbia University's Teachers College. "People are very flexible."

Two spa operators in England have notably effective ways for getting their guests "up" for the fast. Patients at Shrubland Hall Health Clinic are told to think of fasting as a rest, not a deprivation. Lady Julia de Saumarez of Shrubland says, "Rest should be encouraged in every part of the body—muscles, bones and the entire digestive system. When the patient realizes that fasting is in no way analogous to starving, his mental attitude is much more positive and rewarding."

Keki R. Sidhwa, who has supervised about 5,000 fasts ranging from two days to as long as two months at his Shalimar, urges his guests to read up on fasting. Case histories serve to dissolve doubts and fears, and to convey the experience of fasting as a pleasure, not a punishment.

The Buchinger Kliniks in Germany and Spain remind their guests that fasting brings complete relaxation. They tell them to think of fasting as "an utopian vacation," and recommend at least a fortnight of doing without food.

Timing can be an important factor in "getting into it." A dentist in Connecticut who likes to fast 24 to 36 hours twice a week told me he had found it psychologically difficult to start fasting after a dinner and then not to eat again until breakfast two mornings later. He hit upon the easier regimen of starting the fast after breakfast and continuing through lunch the following day. When he gets up that second day, he tells himself he'll be eating again in just a few hours and energetically goes about his business.

One of my correspondents, a concerned citizen, finds the best way to get "in the mood" to skip meals is to remind herself of "disquieting" food facts reported on a NBC television program by Betty Furness, the consumer advocate: "More than 5,500 chemicals are put into our food supply, directly or indirectly, by the food processors [Miss Furness said] . . . the computerized plant, the chemical laboratory, is likely to be the basic source of our food . . . the fact of the matter is, the best scientific minds today are not able to tell us which food chemicals, if any, will cause us bodily harm, when they will strike, and how many of us will be hurt . . . We know there is strong evidence that some of the damage may not show up for years."

It all comes down to convincing yourself it is good for you to fast—which it is!—and get on with it.

Most people do the short fast alone. It's simply something they've chosen to do for a day or two or three, and they manage very well even when others around them are eating and drinking.

Understandably, it is easier for some people to fast by making it a companionable venture, especially if it's for an extended period. You don't have to go away to a spa to have company. Persuade a member of the family or a good friend or a fellow worker to fast with you. This way you can swap progress reports. You'll have a booster to cheer you on. You can check out each other at the scales or before a full-length mirror to see who's losing more weight, who's getting trimmer.

(Maybe someday you'll be able to avail yourself of the new M.I.T. electronic scale. It is so sensitive that the most minuscule fluctuation in weight is registered.

You could stand on such a scale and *see* yourself losing weight from one minute to the next.)

Having a goal can help. If the swimming pool season is only a week away, images of how the "new" you will look in a bathing suit can be a powerful incentive to "shape up" the quickest way. An impending prom or a wedding or a trip to Europe or any other occasion when you'd want to look your best can provide the motivation for launching your fast.

Here is another suggestion that works with many of my patients. Figure out how much time you will save by not eating. My co-author Eugene Boe finds preparing for a business trip eats up so much time that he fasts the two or three days prior to departure in order to save about four hours each day.

Think of all the money you also save by not eating.

There are exciting ways to spend the saved time and money.

Why not reward yourself for being so good? One ingenious device is to pay yourself for each pound you lose. The reward money could easily come out of the money you save on food bills with every day you fast. By fasting just one day a week, you save nearly 15 percent of your weekly food bill.

The financial incentive also seems to work very well in research projects. At the Veterans Administration Hospital in Salt Lake City, subjects in an experiment were paid to fast. The men reportedly threw themselves into the project with great fervor.

Another novel approach for getting "set" comes from a friend who has fasted many times. She suggests using my refeeding schedule *in reverse*. That is, if she plans to fast for three days, she allots herself three days of "training." She begins with my Day Three postfast menu (see page 29) and day by day reduces rations (see pages 28-27) until the fourth day—the first day of a three-day fast. A three-day fast preceded by the three-day "refeeding" program leads to an impressive weight loss and, I might add, a trimmer figure.

Generally, the initial experience with fasting breeds the desire to do it again. And again and again.

Bernarr Macfadden, an indefatigable exponent of fasting, once remarked, "A weekly fast is necessary to insure the continuous possession of the vigor and vitality we all crave. Intoxicating health is indeed life's greatest treasure and any effort made to acquire it pays rich dividends." Mr. Macfadden was still parachute-jumping at the age of 83.

The best "psyching up" stratagem has to be the simple reminder to yourself that fasting is good for you. It produces results at a pace and of a quality not obtainable with any of the diets that come along every season and are widely tried and found wanting.

At last count there were 27,960 different methods for losing weight on file in Washington. Most of them have a brief vogue and are abandoned. Fasting has outlived them all.

4.
Business As Usual

For me a day of fasting is like any other day. I go about my usual busy routine, seeing patients and making my hospital rounds. The only difference is that I don't eat. By not eating I find I have extra time to catch up on my reading and writing. I also have increased stores of energy. (I was not surprised to read that a group of young men in a University of Minnesota experiment *improved* their performance at *hard* work with *periodic* fasts.)

Every healthy person who fasts for a day or two or for many days should be able to go about normal social and work routines—"business as usual."

There is no psychological or physiological reason for cutting back on activity. Fasting for short periods is perfectly compatible with a full work load and an active participation in play. You will instinctively know if you have to cut back a bit.

The very definition of fasting would seem to supply the answer to the question, How does one fast?

The answer is simple: *Stop eating.*

That's it. You don't eat. Nothing could be simpler. Your diet consists of water—and lots of it! At least two quarts a day.

A caution about fasting at home: do not tempt or test yourself needlessly.

Put the thought of food out of your mind. Skip the food pages in newspapers or magazines. Don't riffle through cookbooks and menu files. Walk briskly by restaurants without pausing to examine menus posted in

windows. Bypass supermarkets and bakeries and delica-
tessens and ice cream parlors.

If you are a homemaker, you cannot possibly escape all encounters with food. You will probably have
to go on preparing meals for the rest of the family.
This presents a challenge, but not an insuperable one. I
know a mistress of the house who even hosts lovely
dinner parties while fasting. In many households where
the homemaker is fasting, another family member takes
over the chores of shopping and cooking.

Lorraine Orr, owner-moderator of the syndicated
radio program (over 400 stations) called "Good Living," tells me she is able when she fasts to put in several
extra hours in the office while her husband takes over in
the kitchen. If the Orrs are having guests, he serves her
during the cocktail hour a Perrier "highball" that looks
for all the world like the vodka and soda she normally
has. During a fast, Mrs. Orr finds it "a pleasant surprise" that she has high energy even at the end of a
long dinner party.

A 29-year-old free-lance writer and children's magazine editor, Denise Van Lear, fasted several times
during a heavy writing project. She was greatly helped
by an imaginative friend who surprised her with a
"grande bouffe." He set the dining table with the usual
cutlery and napery and brought on large pitchers,
crystal goblets, soup bowls, and cups—all filled to the
brim with water. He then touched a match to tall, per-
fumed candles. "At that moment I loved him more
than ever," she later told me. She had such renewed
gusts of energy that she took to scrubbing and cleaning
her whole house from stem to stern; she had a compul-
sion to make it as "immaculate" as the fast was making
her. She would bound out of bed at six o'clock in the
morning ready to tackle anything.

Since he began fasting on a regular basis, the director
of the television department of a busy talent agency
said he has never performed better in his work. "I have
so much energy, I always feel great. I am a very happy
man," he told me. "I've got everyone here fasting now."

On a trip to the West Coast, I read in the *Los Angeles Times* of a construction engineer who enjoyed a ten-day fast while his fellow workers and family all continued to eat ravenously. He socialized with "the boys" at lunch over a glass of water on the rocks. At the dinner table he savored the same for his "entree," while the rest of the family packed away "tons of food." After dinner he jogged his usual two miles. The *Times* reported he lost the desired amount of weight "with no effort at all."

Barbara Pinsof, A.S.I.D., who heads her own interior design firm in Glencoe, Illinois, got up each morning of a five-day fast with "more bounce and energy than customary." She astounded herself with her ease at fasting. "I turned off the hunger response totally," she said, "and felt very well. Never hungry, I turned out a tremendous amount of work that week—and lost 12 pounds in the bargain."

A woman interviewed by *W*, the Fairchild weekly which reports on high fashion and the antics of "society," reported: "I don't lead a quiet life while fasting; I just continue being as busy as usual. I fast when I have something important coming up, or when I'm bored, or to clean out my system. Fasting gets me quite excited. It must be nervous energy."

A newspaper woman in the South gets "tons and tons" of things done while fasting. During a single "lunch" hour she ran errands that had been accumulating for weeks. (She also became aware of the hordes on the street who "are always stuffing their face with cold drinks, potato chips, candy, and peanuts—in public yet.") In San Francisco, an entertainment response analyst, Sebastian Stone, uses his extra hours to meditate, to get in touch with his system, nerves, and tensions.

Feelings of fasting-induced euphoria or light-headedness can distort perception. This raises the important question of whether to drive a car during a fast. There are differences of opinion on the subject. I know of a man in Denver who deliberately fasts during a three- or four-day automobile trip so that he won't have to pull into "greasy spoons" along the way. And I know of a spa where the guests are permitted to take day-long motor trips in the historic surrounding countryside.

I see no objection to driving during a short fast if the person is in average good health and is not fasting to alleviate an illness. Performance at the wheel should be keener with the increased alertness.

The body usually adapts itself easily to the fasting experience. Most people breeze through even an extended fast without experiencing discomfort, since the process of nutrition continues as though food were still being consumed. Some fasters report fleeting headache or nausea or faintness or dizziness or palpitations as the body rids itself of waste.

Many working people I know fast in the pursuit of self-improvement. They use their meal hours and meal money to attend adult education courses, redecorate their apartment, or take tennis or language or music lessons. Some go to a popular movie over the lunch hour, when queues aren't as long as after work.

Single people who are accustomed to cooking for themselves appreciate fasting as a way of escaping from the boredom and nuisance of shopping, cooking, and cleaning up for one.

5.

How to Lose Weight Without Eating—and Keep It Off

We are spending billions annually to lose weight. But despite the peer—and medical—pressures to shed our excess weight, we are heavier today than we were 15 years ago.

And the incidence of obesity is still increasing, according to Columbia University's Institute of Human Nutrition. Women are gaining weight at a faster rate than men, particularly women in the 30–40 age range: 40 percent of all women in this group are now classified as obese.

Thirty-five percent of *all* Americans (including children) are overweight and 20 percent are obese. (Obesity—which is defined as being 20 percent over one's preferred weight—is our number one health problem.) The obese person has a 40 percent greater likelihood of dying from heart-related diseases than a person of a preferred weight. Anyone 25 pounds overweight is in effect carrying around a 25-pound bag everywhere he goes.

America has imprisoned itself in a tunnel of fat. This has been true from the beginning of the republic. Benjamin Franklin, who knew whence he spoke, noted, "I saw few die of hunger, but of eating? 100,000!" Too many mouths still act as litter baskets and garbage dumps.

The change in our diet in recent times is reflected in these grim statistics: between 1929 and 1958, per capita consumption of fresh fruits and vegetables declined 30 percent while consumption of processed foods increased 152 percent.

The nation badly needs to go on a diet. It should do something drastic about excessive, unattractive, life-threatening fat. It should get rid of it in the quickest way possible—by fasting.

How much weight can you lose on a fast?

A great deal. More than you could on any kind of diet.

The rate at which you lose weight is generally in proportion to the degree you are overweight. You can lose up to 5 pounds on a one-day fast, up to 10 pounds on a weekend fast, and from 12 to 20 pounds or more on a week-long fast. Men, because they tend to be larger and heavier, lose weight more quickly than women.

Given the mathematical equation of weight loss— we must burn up 3,500 more calories than we consume in order to lose one pound—you might well ask how is it conceivable to lose so much weight so rapidly. The explanation is simple. Our body is about 70 percent water. Eating causes the retention of fluid. When we stop eating, large amounts of water are eliminated from the body. The scale is pound-blind: it treats a pound of water the way it treats a pound of fat. Each weighs exactly the same.

During the "first fine careless rapture" of a fast, pounds drop off rapidly. Understandably, progress is not quite as impressive thereafter.

In the beginning the body loses accumulated water. This accounts for the considerable weight loss. Then it begins to "burn" its fat, a much slower process. After a week or more, the rate of weight loss decreases to about a pound a day. The body is now getting its nutrients from its well-stocked pantry of "preserves." This "pantry" is ample to supply all nutrition needs for several weeks—and sometimes longer for the obese —without drawing on any of its emergency rations.

Too many people in their desperation to rid themselves instantly of extra pounds choose methods that are as dangerous as being overweight itself. Chief among these methods are the "anti-appetite" pills, which are gulped down indiscriminately, and restrictive diets that allow only one type of food. How much better—and how much more effective—it is to take the health-promoting approach of a fast!

The late Director of the Federal Bureau of Investigation, J. Edgar Hoover, was known to abhor flab on his agents. In a thinly disguised novel about the F.B.I. called *Don't Embarrass the Bureau,* agents of the bureau are instructed to fast in advance of a visit from The Director. One of the officers tells his men, "I expect to be looking at some pretty lean bodies around here within the next few weeks. There's absolutely no reason why we should be criticized for something like excess weight. I've been told a person can lose as much as 20 pounds in one week if need be."

Andrew Unger has written in *Moneysworth,* "Compared to a standard program like that of Weight Watchers or Dr. Atkins, fasting is the superior form of weight control. A typical fast is for the goal of losing 12 to 15 pounds. Think of it as losing a Don Carter bowling ball."

The insurance companies have been telling us we might live a lot longer if we weighed considerably less than even the recommended weights on most charts. The insurance companies, as we all know, are geared to the profit motive. I should think it would make good business sense for them to underwrite fasting treatments for obese people rather than pay out policy money for premature death caused by such obesity-related complications as high blood pressure, diabetes, or elevated cholesterol levels.

Every day's mail brings cheering accounts from correspondents who have overcome their weight problems through fasting. Here is a sampling of "case histories":

I was able to lose 22 pounds within eight days. On two subsequent fasts I lost another 25 pounds. My wife has also lost weight faster by fasting than by any other means. Fasting for short periods of time is certainly the fastest and most predictable method I know. . . .—Dr. M. N. N., Perth Amboy, New Jersey.

I was severely overweight, about 100 pounds or so. I was able to take off all 100 pounds. . . . (Why is it that we lavish so much money on the maintenance of our automobiles to keep them from conking out and so little concern on keeping our bodies from conking out?)—A. G. G., Manhattan, Kansas.

In two weeks I lost 27 pounds and all my funny little aches and pains disappeared.—G. F., Taunton, Massachusetts.

I was feeling sluggish, sleepy and overweight, and ready to retire from my insurance business when I went on my first fast. After seven days I had lost 23 pounds and was able to return to my office and work a full 14-hour day as I hadn't done for years. I now fast at least a day a week. . . .—S. G. R., Oxnard, California.

On my most recent birthday, which coincided with Oxfam's Fast Day, I determined I must lose excess weight and take stock of myself. I decided to fast, and now have lost over 20 pounds. I did yoga exercises at the same time—mainly upside down ones for circulation: headstands, shoulder stands, and "the plow."—Ms. S. R. C., Iowa City, Iowa.

As a nurse I should have known better. But I let myself go all the way up to 245 pounds. I went on a four-day fast and lost 15 pounds. To be continued. . . .—Ms. B. A., Trenton, New Jersey.

One of the most satisfying rewards of being the author of *Fasting: The Ultimate Diet* was to learn that the regimen set down in the book had inspired weight-reduction programs on a company-wide basis. At Intermatic, Inc., an electrical products manufacturing concern in Spring Grove, Illinois, a "Diet Derby" was instituted. Each entrant was to be paid three dollars for each pound lost, providing at least 15 pounds were lost in a year. The company made no recommendation on how to lose weight. Each employee was allowed to pursue her or his own method; there seemed to be as many methods as there were reducers. Some ate only candy bars. Others consumed only salad dressings. A few tried yoga. And there were those who believed more things are wrought by prayer than this world dreams of.

About halfway through the program, Intermatic's president, Jim Miller, noted that the participants were disappointed with their progress. Not many pounds were being shed, or kept off. At this point he distributed a copy of *Fasting: The Ultimate Diet* to each person still in the program. Here is what he told me:

The reactions to your book were very favorable. As one person and then another tried fasting and reported that the desire for food diminished greatly after the first day, others were encouraged to try it, too. When I gave the awards at the end of the program, most of the men and women with whom I talked attributed their successes to "the ultimate diet." There was agreement that fasting is much easier than dieting, and that fasting gives immediate results.

There was no doubt, from my observation, that those who had succeeded in fasting had a sense of accomplishment and a much improved outlook. They reported having a sense of "renewal." There is a psychological impact as a result of fasting beyond merely loss of weight.

The 137 employees in the Intermatic Derby collectively "lost" more than half a ton. In addition, there was the auxiliary benefit of the appreciable drop in blood-pressure levels which always accompany a fast.

As a result of the Diet Derby and the national attention it attracted, Mr. Miller is "convinced a major segment of our population has a great desire to be thin. It seems to me a very large number of young people in particular are carrying excessive weight and they feel somehow it is unfair. We live in a permissive society where the child can get away from his parents, his teachers, and even his church—only Mother Nature seems to demand self-discipline."

I agree with the Intermatic president when he says that far more important than the money the "losers" won are the *years* they've won—the years added to their lives. Overweight can be *very* dangerous. Anyone who rids himself of excess weight is a much healthier and more effective person.

Once you resume eating, some weight gain *naturally* occurs. The body retains fluid, which translates into weight because of the sodium content in food. For a time after any fast this will be more weight than is metabolically balanced for the amount of calories being consumed.

The best way to keep your weight down after the initial fast and to keep reaching new low levels is to make fasting a way of life.

If you fast principally to lose weight, the ultimate goal should be to keep off the pounds you lose. Fast on a regular basis: one day every week, or every weekend, or three days every month, or even one-week to ten-day periods twice a year.

Between fasts, try to keep caloric consumption in alignment with caloric needs. Such a program should lead to successive lower readings on the scale.

A return to a previously unhealthy life-style can take away the blessings gained through fasting. This is a fact I cannot over-emphasize.

6.

After-the-Fast Menus

When you start to eat again, you must not burden the digestive system—now cleansed and rested—with too much food or the wrong kind of food.

When you have fasted for even a few days, your system will require less food than you had been accustomed to eating. (You will not have accumulated hunger or appetite.)

After a longer fast—of a week or more—the body is enlightened. It puts appetite into alignment with the body's *real* needs for energy. The probability is you will now consume only as much food as your body burns.

In the words of a veteran faster, "A fast heightens awareness of the individual's integral relationship to the nourishment that feeds the body."

Gorging food after the fast or trying to compensate for "lost meals" could have lamentable consequences. At the very least you would surely regain weight you had shed. You could also become ill.

The wise person eases into a sensible refeeding program. Easy does it if you want to continue feeling wonderful and to keep your weight at or near its new low level.

In effect, the body is re-educated by a fast. It "unlearns" habits of overeating and "polluting." It is "born again." It inclines toward a natural state. It wants only as much food as is required for maintenance. It prefers the kinds of food that are natural to the taste and harmonious to the digestive system.

My new after-the-fast eating schedule is an agreeable

and palatable alternative to the refeeding program that appeared in *Fasting: The Ultimate Diet*. The menu plans are intended to keep your weight at—or below —its post-fasting level. They are also designed to provide a healthy, nutritious, high-energy interlude between the completion of the fast and the resumption of regular meals. They are balanced and complete in all the essential nutrients.

Throughout the after-the-fast diet you may drink as much water as you wish. *You should drink at least one quart of water every day.*

It is advisable to eat slowly and to chew carefully. (Good advice anytime.)

You should not add salt to your food.

You should adhere to the refeeding schedule for the same number of days you fasted. If you fasted five days, for example, you should follow the schedule through Day Five.

Most people who fast of course continue their normal work routine. It is suggested they prepare their refeeding meals on arising in the morning. Meals to be eaten during the day can be put into thermal containers and taken along to the job.

When you return to a regular eating pattern, the likelihood is that you will be eating more selectively and austerely, which is all to the good.

The Day One Menu

The day's menu consists of one pint of boiled water mixed with one pint of grape juice or orange juice or apricot juice.

Sip two or three teaspoons of the mixture every ten to fifteen minutes throughout the day, finishing the full quart by bedtime.

The Day Two Menu

The menu consists of undiluted grape juice or orange juice or apricot juice.

Drink half a cup (four ounces) of the juice on arising and an additional half a cup every two hours until bedtime. You will drink one quart of the fruit juice if you are up 14 hours today.

The Day Three Menu

The menu of five meals consists of one quart of yogurt and one pound of apples.

Wash and grate the apples, and mix with the yogurt.

Divide the combination into five equal meals.

Eat a meal every three hours, preferably at 9:00 A.M., noon, 3:00 P.M., 6:00 P.M., and 9:00 P.M.

The Day Four Menu

The menu of five meals consists of one quart of yogurt, one pound of apples, and one-half pound of carrots.

Wash and grate the apples and carrots, and mix with the yogurt.

Divide the combination into five equal meals.

Eat a meal every three hours, preferably at 9:00 A.M., noon, 3:00 P.M., 6:00 P.M., and 9:00 P.M.

The Day Five Menu

The menu of five meals consists of one and one-quarter cups of yogurt, one-quarter pound of apples, one-quarter pound of carrots, one teaspoon of honey, a vegetable salad (described below), and two walnuts.

Wash and grate the apples and carrots, mix with the yogurt, and add the teaspoon of honey and the walnuts. Divide the combination into five equal meals. Eat at the same hours as on Days Three and Four: 9:00 A.M., noon, 3:00 P.M., 6:00 P.M., and 9:00 P.M.

At the noon meal, have also a vegetable salad consisting of one boiled potato, one cup of raw fresh chopped cabbage, and one chopped onion—dressed with one tablespoon of vegetable oil.

The Day Six Menu

The menu of four meals consists of one and one-quarter cups of yogurt, one-quarter pound of apples, one-third pound of carrots, two teaspoons of honey, two walnuts, one-third pound of farmer cheese, and a vegetable salad (described below).

Wash and grate the apples and carrots, mix with the yogurt, and add the honey and the walnuts. Divide the combination into four equal meals. Eat a meal every four hours, preferably at 9:00 A.M., 1:00 P.M., 5:00 P.M., and 9:00 P.M.

At the morning meal, add the farmer cheese.

At the 1:00 P.M. meal, add a vegetable salad consisting of one boiled potato, one cup of raw fresh chopped cabbage, and one chopped onion—dressed with one tablespoon of vegetable oil.

The Day Seven Menu

The menu of four meals consists of one and one-quarter cups of yogurt, one-quarter pound of apples, one-third pound of carrots, two teaspoons of honey, two walnuts, two-thirds pound of farmer cheese, a vegetable salad, and a cup of oatmeal or buckwheat topped with milk.

Wash and grate the apples and carrots, mix with the yogurt, and add the honey and the walnuts. Divide the combination into four equal meals. Follow the same meal schedule as for Day Six: 9:00 A.M., 1:00 P.M., 5:00 P.M., and 9:00 P.M.

At each meal have one-fourth of the farmer cheese.

At the morning meal, have the oatmeal or buckwheat topped with milk.

At the 1:00 P.M. meal, have the vegetable salad consisting of the same ingredients as that for Day Five or Six.

The Day Eight Menu

The same menu and schedule of four meals as Day Seven.

The Day Nine Menu

The same menu and schedule of four meals as Day Seven, except for the addition of one tablespoon of sour cream mixed with the day's portion of farmer cheese.

The Day Ten Menu

The same menu and schedule of four meals as Day Nine, plus a cup of vegetable soup at the 1:00 P.M. meal.

The Day Eleven Menu

The same menu and schedule of four meals as Day Ten.

The Day Twelve Menu

The same menu and schedule of four meals as Day Eleven, with the addition of three teaspoons of vegetable oil and a pint of orange, grape, or apricot juice.

At the morning, 1:00 P.M., and 5:00 P.M. meals, have a teaspoon of vegetable oil. (You may wish to add the vegetable oil to your vegetable salad.)

At each meal have one four-ounce serving of the fruit juice.

The Day Thirteen Menu and Beyond

Continue the menu and schedule of four meals of Day Twelve for as many additional days as are necessary—that is, if you fasted for fifteen days, you should adhere to the Day Twelve diet for three additional days.

My after-the-fast schedule is one of several in popular use. Two estimable alternative refeeding programs
were kindly supplied for presentation in this book by
Joy and Robert Gross, who operate the Pawling Health
Manor in Hyde Park, New York. The programs are
appropriate for the seven-day refeeding period after a
week-long fast. Amounts may be adjusted to individual
desire. (I do not use either of these programs for
breaking the fast.)

First day after the fast
4 ounces fresh orange juice mixed with 4 ounces water.
Sip slowly, every three hours.

OR:
Breakfast: 1 grapefruit
Lunch: 6 ounces clear vegetable broth
Dinner: 1 grapefruit

Second day after the fast
Breakfast: 8 ounces fresh orange juice
Lunch: 1 small piece watermelon
Dinner: 2 oranges

OR
Breakfast: 8 ounces fresh tomato and celery juice
Lunch: 1 pound fresh grapes
Dinner: 8–10 ounces vegetable broth

Third day after the fast
Breakfast: 8 ounces fresh carrot and celery juice
Lunch: 1 or 2 ripe tomatoes, couple of stalks
              celery, 3 ounces pot cheese
Dinner: Medium-sized vegetable salad, baked
              potato

OR:
Breakfast: 1 grapefruit
Lunch: Several slices ripe fresh pineapple, 8–10
             strawberries
Dinner: Green salad, steamed baby peas, 3 ounces
             pot cheese

Fourth day after the fast
Breakfast: 8–10 ounces fresh grapefruit juice, 3
             ounces sunflower seeds
Lunch: 1 ripe banana, 1 ripe pear, ½ cup raisins
Dinner: 8 ounces carrot and celery juice, medium-
             sized green salad, baked potato, steamed
             asparagus

OR:
Breakfast: 1 grapefruit, 1 orange
Lunch: 1 large ripe tomato, 4 ounces alfalfa
             sprouts, 2 stalks celery, steamed whole
             green beans
Dinner: Medium-sized salad, medium portion
             steamed brown or wild rice, steamed
             zucchini squash

Fifth day after the fast
Breakfast: 1 medium-sized piece watermelon
Lunch: 8 ounces vegetable soup, 3 or 4 ounces
             cottage cheese, several leaves romaine
             lettuce
Dinner: Medium-sized green salad, 1 ripe tomato,
             3 or 4 ounces sprouts, ½ avocado

OR:
Breakfast: 8 ounces carrot and celery juice, 3 ounces
             pine nuts
Lunch: 3 or 4 large nectarines
Dinner: Medium-sized green salad, baked potato,
             steamed broccoli

Sixth day after the fast

Breakfast: Fresh strawberries, 3 ounces raw cashew
               butter
Lunch: 1 or 2 ripe mangoes, 8 ounces fresh ripe
               blueberries
Dinner: Large green salad, steamed lima beans,
               ½ avocado

OR:

Breakfast: 1 or 2 grapefruits
Lunch: 2 ripe bananas, 3 ounces natural dates,
               1 pear
Dinner: Large green salad, steamed eggplant with
               tomatoes, 3 or 4 ounces pot cheese

Seventh day after the fast

Breakfast: Ripe papaya (as much as desired)
Lunch: Fresh blueberries, 1 or 2 ripe peaches, 3
               ounces ricotta cheese
Dinner: Finger salad—romaine lettuce leaves,
               celery, carrot sticks, green pepper slices,
               endive; steamed yellow squash, steamed
               kasha

OR:

Breakfast: 5 or 6 soaked jumbo prunes
Lunch: 6 or 8 ounces fresh vegetable soup, fresh
               celery sticks, 3 ounces imported Swiss
               cheese
Dinner: Large green salad, vegetable casserole—
               alternating layers of ripe tomatoes, egg-
               plant, green peppers, potato, parsley, in
               baking dish. (Soybean oil may be used in
               bottom of pan and if liquid is needed,
               celery juice may be used.)

7.
After the After-the-Fast Menus

You have shed many pounds during your fast and approached or arrived at approximately your ideal weight.

From my experience, there is no doubt you will have a much better chance for permanent weight control after fasting than after any diet. The system now *wants* to reject food in excess of the needs of the body.

You should now be able to gain a new perspective on food and a new relationship to food that can keep you from overeating or from eating undesirable foods. Fasting and a sensible refeeding program have led to this desideratum.

The after the after-the-fast diet should consist of modest amounts of all fruits and vegetables currently available. It should favor fresh fruits and vegetables, whole grains and cereals, nuts and seeds, poultry and fish. It should be sparing of meat, sweets, and fats, and free of any food containing sugar, and it should be low in salt.

There are many healthful diets providing "three squares" a day that still allow for weight control. Here is one basic menu I recommend—and basically follow:

Breakfast: Half a grapefruit or an orange or the juice of either. A cooked or a granola-type cereal plus one tablespoon of unprocessed bran five mornings a week, one egg the other two mornings. One butterless piece of whole wheat or rye toast with honey. A cup of café au lait consisting of one-third cup of coffee and two-thirds cup of boiled milk, or herbal tea with lemon.

Lunch: A cup of plain yogurt with nuts and figs or raisins two or three days each week. Fruit or a vegetable salad on the other days.

Dinner: Fish or fowl. A huge bowl of salad with lots of vegetables. A baked potato. For dessert, a piece of cheese and an apple or a pear.

For a great many people, fasting leads to a vegetarian life. Most fasting retreats serve only vegetarian meals after the refeeding program. They urge their guests to adopt new dietary habits, all-vegetarian if possible, on returning home. Some prepare menu plans for the departing guests.

Without departing from the conviction that diet, where possible, should be individually tailored, Shrubland Hall Health Clinic in England makes available to patients on departure a general diet sheet. (I do not use this sheet.) The advice it gives is this:

On Waking:

Hot or cold water with lemon and honey. *This is essential.*

Breakfast:

N.B. This is the most important meal of the day. On no account leave it out.

Either one-half grapefruit or one orange or apple.

Select one:

1. Boiled egg, one crispbread with a little butter (one-half ounce total daily allowance).

2. Four ounces plain yogurt with wheat germ or bran and honey (one ounce total daily allowance).

3. One-half cup Muesli *well soaked* in boiling water *or* fruit juice, *not* milk.

4. Prunes (soaked in hot water for 24 hours). All-bran *or* plain bran for extra bowel movement should be added if required.

5. Two lean rashers grilled bacon and one tomato.

(The above may be alternated.)

One cup China or herbal tea or coffee (not instant) *or* small glass *fresh* fruit juice. No milk (one-half cup allowed daily *if absolutely necessary*). No sugar (non-caloric sweetener if essential).

Mid-morning:
Nothing if possible. Otherwise choose one:
1. Small glass fresh fruit or vegetable juice.
2. Cup of tea or coffee. No milk or sugar.
3. One cup marmite or soup. One low-calorie fruit or vegetable, e.g., apple, carrot, celery, *if you need it.*

Luncheon:
First course (if desired)
Select one: consommé, tomato juice, grapefruit, melon.
Main Course
Mixed salad containing as many different raw vegetables as possible. Select six from: lettuce, watercress, fennel, grated raw cabbage, grated white cabbage, grated carrot, grated raw beetroot, chicory, endive, onion, cucumber, raw mushroom, shredded raw spinach, mustard and cress, celery, radish, green pepper, grated celeriac.
One teaspoon cider vinegar *or l*emon juice for dressing if desired.
Select one from: boiled egg (total weekly allowance of four), six prawns or shrimp, two ounces grated cheese *or* milled nuts, four ounces cottage cheese, small baked potato (may be included twice weekly), avocado pear.
Third Course
Two crispbread or one slice wholemeal brown bread. Very little butter. Tea *or* coffee (see breakfast).
Do not have cheese, fruit, or eggs twice in the same meal.

Tea Time:
One or two cups China or herbal tea (with lemon if desired).
One teaspoon honey or brown sugar is beneficial at this time of day and may be taken in addition to the daily allowance.
No coffee, no milk, nothing to eat.

Dinner:
  First Course
  None if taken at luncheon; otherwise select from
luncheon choices.
  Main Course
  Select two vegetables from: carrots, parsnips, celery,
onions, leeks, French beans, Brussels sprouts, cauli-
flower, spinach, broccoli, tomatoes, marrow squash,
cabbage, green peppers, eggplant, sea kale, mushrooms,
courgettes. (These must be boiled or steamed, grilled
where applicable, never fried.)
  Salt may be used in cooking but very little added
afterwards.
  Select one medium portion from: two ounces grilled
liver, three ounces lamb chop, three ounces veal, three
ounces roast chicken, two ounces lamb, three ounces
turkey, four ounces steamed or grilled whitefish such as
cod, sole, plaice, fresh haddock. No sauces. No gravy.
(Cheese or egg dishes are suitable alternatives.)
  Third Course (if required)
  Select one fresh fruit from: peach, apple, melon,
plums, apricots, pear, cherries, pineapple, black or red
currants, blackberries, orange, gooseberries.
  Beverage
  One or two glasses of dry wine with dinner, if abso-
lutely necessary for social or business reasons.
  Otherwise, for the purpose of this diet, regard all
alcoholic beverages as unsuitable and avoid them.
  Do not have the bedtime drink if you have had wine.
  You may reverse the suggested luncheon and dinner.

Bedtime:
  Optional drink. Hot water flavored with honey and
cider vinegar or lemon. Herbal tea, vecon, or marmite.
(Avoid stimulants such as coffee and China or India
tea on retiring. You do not need a milky drink.)

Unsuitable foods:
  White bread, white sugar, cakes, pastries, puddings,
biscuits, white rice, spaghetti, pastas in general, thick
soups, sauces, gravies, olive oil, dressings, milk, milk
shakes, fat meat such as pork, sausage, beefsteak, fat

fish such as pilchards, herrings, sardines, breakfast cereals (except Muesli), jams, marmalade, syrup, canned foods, dried foods, sandwiches, snacks, chocolate, sweets, ice cream, cream, dried fruits such as dates, figs, sultanas, prunes, apricots, rhubarb, bananas. (Peas, potatoes, brown sugar, honey, ham, bacon, butter, margarine only in amounts indicated in the diet.)

The Shrubland diet, the dietician tells the guest, has been carefully balanced to meet all nutritional requisites for good health and a sense of well-being. You are strongly advised to adhere to it and not to tamper with it in any way. It is designed to give maximum variety and generous freedom of choice according to individual taste. Therefore, you should find it socially acceptable and personally satisfying to your appetite; your family, social, and business requirements can be met without preventing you from following the diet strictly. Easy preparation and food prices have also been taken into careful consideration.

Again, the above diet and advice are Shrubland's, not mine.

8.

The Adequacy of Vegetarian Diets

Today, there is increasing interest in vegetarianism. The reasons are various. First, there is the continuing problem of inflation, which is bringing higher and higher costs of food in general and meat in particular. Also, there is a growing sensitivity to the hunger and food shortages confronting most of the world's population. And there is the increasing suspicion there might be a link between some illnesses and a diet heavy on meats.

The person who fasts frequently comes to prefer the vegetarian regimen.

This reorientation raises the question, can vegetarian diets satisfy nutritional needs?

The word *vegetarian* is *not*—as one might presume —derived from the word *vegetable,* but from the Latin *vegettus,* which means "whole, sound, fresh, lively."

All vegetarian diets exclude meat, poultry, and fish. But vegetarian diets differ significantly in what they do contain.

The four most common variations of vegetarianism are:

1. A pure or strict "vegan" diet. It excludes all foods of meat-poultry-fish *origin* (eggs, milk, cheese, ice cream, yogurt, etc.).

2. The ovo-lacto vegetarian diet. It allows eggs and dairy products.

3. A lacto vegetarian diet. It permits dairy products but excludes eggs.

4. A fruitarian diet. It is restricted to raw and dried fruits, nuts, honey, and olive oil.

Large populations of the world have subsisted on

diets that are essentially, if not literally, vegetarian. According to the Scriptures, the human diet was to consist of fruits, seeds, and nuts. Later, herbs and vegetables were "approved." The Creator said, "Behold, I have given you every herb-bearing seed that is upon the face of all the Earth and every tree in which is the fruit of a tree-yielding seed, to you it shall be for meat."

The latest official statistic—it goes back to a Gallup poll taken in 1943—indicated that in the United States alone there were 3-million vegetarians. The present concern for ecology and a contented, harmonious life —combined with new nutritional knowledge—has boosted that total, I would guess, to at least 12-million.

Despite the fact man has survived perfectly well throughout history on fleshless food, there is periodically raised the concern as to the amount and proper kind of protein that vegetarian diets provide.

The quantity and the quality of protein are a concern in *any* diet. The quality of protein is determined by the kinds of amino acids—the building blocks of protein—the food contains. Eight of the 23 constituent amino acids in protein are considered vitally important to the diet. They are referred to as "essential." They are available in plant sources. Killing of animals for protein is indeed an arrogant exploitation of Earth's finite resources.

Soybeans and chick peas are rich in high-grade protein. So are lentils, nuts, and seeds. Bread, cereal, vegetables, and fruits are not quite as rich. Combining these foods with as much variety as possible provides a diet adequate in protein, and in all other nutrients as well.

Effective protein combinations—which complement each other to make whole or complete proteins—are beans and rice, cereal and milk, and macaroni or other pastas and cheese.

On a vegetarian diet, one must consume larger quantities of food to get adequate nutrients. This does not mean loading up excessively on any foods on the approved list. The recommended wide variety of foods in vegetarian diets is necessary to insure adequate intake of the more-difficult-to-obtain vitamins (folic acid and vitamin B_{12}) and minerals such as calcium and iron.

(For impoverished populations having no choice *but* to be vegetarian, there is the promise of a new type of corn as an answer to protein needs. An international team of scientists has developed a species designated as Opaque-2. It contains large amounts of lysine, which is lacking in ordinary strains of corn. Opaque-2 has about doubled the effective protein content of normal corn, surpassing the amount found even in milk. Sanat K. Majumder, associate professor in the Department of Biological Sciences at Smith College, tells us that under proper agronomic conditions more than 200-million people who live in the tropical corn regions can derive dietary benefit, both quantitatively and qualitatively, from these strains.)

In vegetarian diets, two daily servings of high-protein alternates—peas or beans, nuts, peanut butter, vegetable "steaks," dairy products or eggs—are recommended. If dairy products are not used, calcium and riboflavin can be obtained in adequate amounts by liberal intakes of dark green leafy vegetables and fortified soy milk.

While most of the 4,000,000,000 people on Earth may not be getting enough protein, many affluent Americans are probably consuming too much. Nutritionists once advised that the daily diet should contain one gram for every two pounds of weight. This seems to be in excess of what our body actually requires. The government now says that adults require about 48 grams of protein per day. This figure may be on the high side. Controlled experiments have shown the average person can function perfectly well with protein intakes of only 30 to 35 grams per day. (By the way, even steak rates as "junk food" when it contributes to an excess of protein consumption, in light of the definition that "junk food" is anything the body does not need.)

However many grams of protein we are taking in, we may be much better off if the protein is not from animal sources. Studies by Dr. John W. Berg and others at the National Cancer Institute link colon cancer with high consumption of beef. A study of Seventh-Day Adventist men—most of whom are strict vegetarians—found they have about 75 percent *less* than the expected rate of intestinal and rectal cancer and less than half the expected rate of all types of cancer.

Another study concluded that in populations habitually subsisting on a diet *high* in animal foodstuffs—including dairy products—heart disease was far more prevalent than in vegetarian populations.

Dr. George L. Blackburn, assistant professor of surgery, Harvard Medical School, has gone on record as saying that a vegetarian diet incorporating egg and milk sources of protein "is more than adequate to maintain proper nutrition and resulting health."

Dr. Glenn D. Toppenberg, of New England Memorial Hospital, Stoneham, Massachusetts, goes so far as to claim from personal experience that children can flourish on vegetarian diets. Writing in *The New England Journal of Medicine,* he discusses vegetarian child-raising at first hand: "My three children are now the third generation of my family to have never tasted meat, and it certainly has not been detrimental to our health. My 13-year-old high school boy—6'3" and size-14 shoes—can hardly be accused of retarded physical growth, and all three children are at the top of their classes at school and are socially well adjusted."

Lancet, the British medical journal, supports Dr. Toppenberg's view: ". . . many field trips have shown protein provided by suitable mixtures of vegetable origin enable children to grow as well as children provided with milk and other animal protein."

Corroborating studies involving 112 vegetarian and 88 nonvegetarian adults, adolescents, and pregnant women were reported in the *Journal of Clinical Nutrition* as follows:

1. The average intake of nutrients of *all* groups exceeded those recommended by the National Research Council, with the exception of adolescent "pure" vegetarians.

2. Nonvegetarian adolescents consume more protein, but there is no evidence that an ovo-lacto vegetarian diet failed to provide adequate diet for them or for expectant mothers.

3. There were no significant differences in height, weight, and blood pressures among the groups, but the "pure" vegetarians weighed an average of 20 pounds less.

4. Cholesterol was higher in the nonvegetarian groups. The "pure" vegetarian diet, whatever its shortcomings, is *cholesterol-free*.

Studies conducted by Dr. Frederick Stare of Harvard and Dr. Mervyn G. Hardinge, now dean of Loma Linda (California) School of Health, confirm that vegetarians have consistently lower levels of serum cholesterol than do meat eaters. Meat eaters may also be bothered by poor elimination; food with low fiber content, such as meat, moves sluggishly through the digestive tract.

Many large institutions, such as Smith College, have begun to de-emphasize meat in its meals. At Hampshire College, the director of food services says "food is a subject that students take seriously." At prestigious Stuyvesant High School in New York City, yogurt is now offered in the cafeteria.

Some of our high-circulation periodicals that depend on advertising revenues from meat packers are even endorsing the vegetarian regimen. "The staunchest meat-eaters have come to accept the fact that you don't have to eat red meat, poultry, or fish to get the kind of protein your body needs and can use," according to a *Redbook* article. The magazine published menus for meatless meals providing "balanced" protein. Among the entrees were Brazilian black beans and rice with salsa, two-cheese rice balls, sukiyaki with noodles, linguini with walnut sauce, French bean pot, lentil potato soup, Chinese slivered eggs and mushrooms, cheese-and-potato pie, and sweet and pungent chick peas.

The *Reader's Digest* reprinted an article from *Today's Health* attesting that protein from non-flesh foods can be an adequate nutritional substitute for meat protein. It was observed that "vegetarians are thinner, in better health, with lower blood cholesterol, than their flesh-eating fellow ctitizens."

A *Ladies Home Journal* feature asserted that the heartiest appetites could be satisfied healthfully with ample protein without dependence on meat. The *Journal* published recipes for "main" dishes such as nutty bean loaf, fried stuffed zucchini, Mexican chili baked with soufflé topping, spinach Parmesan pie, and ratatouille crepe stack.

McCall's presented in tabular form "the price of protein," establishing that all the plant-food sources cost but a fraction of meat protein, and concluding that "cutting down on meat wouldn't be a hardship; it can be an exercise in ingenuity to get maximum protein for minimum cost."

Accelerating interest in vegetarianism is a natural consequence of our health-endangered industrial society. Many people—of all ages, not only the Woodstock generation—are seeking alternative life-styles of "purer" foods requiring neither the destruction of animals nor the use of chemical fertilizers and pesticides. They seek a mode of eating that enhances spiritual values and bio-ethics. A 19-year-old woman from Orangevale, California, summed it up in *Seventeen* magazine: "Vegetarianism is a more economical, healthful and ecologically sound way to eat."

9.

The Strenuous Life

Contestants with the training and stamina to participate in long-distance running competitions are typically lean. It is amazing how deceiving appearances can be. These stripped-down, almost cadaverous looking bodies actually have enough reserves to sustain *tremendous* exertion.

Many outstanding runners who are in tip-top condition program fasting into their schedules as faithfully as they do road-work.

Pennsylvanian Park Barner goes without food before long-distance runs. Within a two-week period he ran 36 miles and a double marathon (52½ miles).

A Swede, Erik Ostybe, abstains for several days before a marathon.

Germany's Meinrad Nagele, once severely overweight, credits a series of fasts with helping him "shape up" at the age of 46 and become a winner in the World Veterans games.

Murray Rose, of England, was a gold medal winner in the 1956 and 1960 Olympics. (He was a vegetarian; he had never eaten meat.)

Another English devotee of fasting, Ian Jackson, declared, "I feel better when fasting than when eating. I feel more alert, lighter on my feet, more collected, and calmer than usual." For the *Runner's Diet*, Jackson lyrically recalled what it was like after a week of fasting: ". . . my body was moving effortlessly, gliding along with no urgency. Everything was smooth, mellow and peaceful. My senses were incredibly heightened, finely tuned in. I felt a natural unity with the dark trees and the drifting mist. The sighing of the wind in the pines, the clear bird calls and the occasional creaking of branches seemed to penetrate gently into the very center of my being. With a combination of elation and gratitude, I let my body move on while my mind and my senses touched their home . . . pure awareness of joyful existence."

Dick Gregory, who is in his mid-forties, participated in the Boston Marathon while fasting. As a personal bicentennial celebration, he ran from Los Angeles to New York—a total of 2,980 miles; an average of 50 each day—without taking any solid food.

Nineteen Swedish men, who ranged in ages from 18 to 53, and worked mostly at sedentary jobs, hiked from Kalmar to Stockholm, a distance of more than 300 miles. They ate no food during the 10 days, averaged 30 miles a day, and were in "the best of spirits" on reaching the capital, having taken the whole thing in stride.

Fasting has had its adherents in boxing. To get under the 126-pound maximum weight for the division, featherweight Johnny Chacon fasted for a week to lose 16 pounds. A heavyweight contender, Harry Wills, "the Brown Panther," would fast for a month each Spring in order to lose at least 40 pounds and get into fighting trim.

A famous University of Chicago professor of physiology, Anton Carlson, discovered the endurance and energy of a football team rose markedly after a three- or four-day fast.

It may come as revolutionary news to television viewers of sports and food commercials that *many* professional athletes are foregoing food before competition. The American College of Sports Medicine, based in Madison, Wisconsin, has promulgated the opinion that the traditional pre-game meal is not essential. "In fact, we have observed over many years that some of the truly great athletes ate absolutely nothing before competition."

The hearty pre-game meal is a long-cherished old wives' tale handed down from coach to coach without discernment of its potential harm. Before an event, the traditional thinking went, athletes had to stock up on marbled steaks, mounds of scrambled eggs, gallons of milk, and racks of toast and honey. It is now understood by many coaches the energy needed to digest such a meal is deflected from performance. The food acts as an extra load, contributes to fatigue, and lodges in the stomach long after the event is over.

Ernst van Aaken, a medical doctor who coaches runners, believes frequent fasts lead to greater endurance. "It is necessary," he observes, "to have fasted frequently for at least 24-hour periods in order to perform with a completely empty stomach. Frequent fasts build up carbohydrates in the liver from reserves already present in the organism." He believes endurance activities can be carried on for days with almost no food.

But need I point out athletes (in common with the rest of us) should eat sound, balanced meals containing protein, carbohydrates, and the other essential nutrients when not being called upon for an expenditure of extraordinary amounts of energy. And logically, it seems to be best to eat nothing at all the day *of* and the day *before* the competition. The body does not depend on food consumed just *before* or *during* heightened activity. It performs with the reserves it has accumulated over a period of time. Talk it over with your team doctor or trainer.

During a fast, blood sugar stays on an even keel within the normal range. Those who *eat* experience a rise in blood sugar, which brings on an outpouring of insulin and a lowering of the blood sugar level. For the athlete there may be the accompanying conditioned craving for a Hershey bar or a Gatorade "break."

An article in *Nutrition Reviews* also challenged the notion that athletes should pack away a feast before going into action. At the same time it questioned the

wisdom of carbohydrate-loading athletes in training,
pointing out that its effectiveness is doubtful. As a matter of fact, the fasting process releases ketones into the
bloodstream, blunting hunger and providing a source
of energy for metabolism.

(We are of course talking throughout this chapter
about mature, fully developed athletes—not growing
grade school or high school youngsters. *Young people
during their growth period should never fast except in a
medically controlled situation.*)

With the whole world now sports wild, it is time we
discard many myths concerning the care and feeding
of athletes. In reading a provocative book entitled
Food for Fitness, I found myself in solid agreement
again and again with its iconoclastic views. The book,
by the way, was published by World Books, a California publishing enterprise specializing in books and
manuals on active and intense sports: cross-country skiing, swimming, bicycling, running, gymnastics, the mar-
tial arts, canoeing, hiking, and rafting.

"Nowhere is superstition more flagrantly and un-
questionably adhered to than in diets," declares *Food
for Fitness.* It then proceeds to slaughter many a sacred
cow:

"Every body needs milk." Absolutely not so. In fact,
there are many people, including a large segment of the
white population and an even greater percentage of the
black population, who cannot digest it.

"Every body needs bread." Again not so. And again
there are those who literally cannot stomach it. Their
systems are unable to produce enzymes necessary to
break down starch and protein simultaneously.

"Steak for breakfast is best on game day." Steak
at that time is a drag, not a lift. Its protein doesn't
convert into energy quickly enough to be helpful. It
also overburdens the elimination system at a time when
it is already overworked with heavy perspiring.

"Candy bars give you a boost." They do—for a matter of moments—and then drop you like a runaway

express elevator. "The entire 'quick energy' myth is a giant rip-off invented by the very industry that led you to eat things that make you feel sluggish in the first place."

"Protein gives you a quick lift before an event." In the energy derby, protein comes in last. Of all nutrients, it takes the most time to digest. Fruit sugars, starchy foods, and fats give a quicker "pick-me-up." (*Seventeen* magazine has said, "The traditional steak dinner or pre-game breakfast to turn players into dynamos is nothing but a high-priced myth.")

Even the American Dietetic Association dismisses the notion of high-protein intake as a *sine qua non* for athletes. "Protein utilization does not increase during exercise when fat and carbohydrate contribute sufficient energy," the A.D.A. maintains. "Diets high in protein and protein supplements have been advocated for athletes on the premise that body muscle is protein and an ingestion of an excess of protein would stimulate muscle growth to improve strength."

(*The Physician and Sportsmedicine* magazine reports studies in animals and humans have not demonstrated any benefits from eating excessive amounts of protein. "In fact, one of the most impressive developments in clinical nutrition has been the treatment of chronic renal disease by *lowering* protein intake." The periodical asks, "If such good results are possible by restricting the intake of protein, is excessive protein intake healthy for normal human beings? Is there perhaps even danger in over-consumption of protein?")

"Drinking anything is bad before, during, or after strenuous exercise." Nonsense! Athletes have been known to die of dehydration. Body temperature soars during dehydration, bringing on the threat of a fatal heat stroke. In less than an hour, athletes can sweat away dangerous amounts of fluid. They can suffer dizziness, nausea, and a dangerously elevated pulse rate if they don't replenish themselves constantly. Don't worry about bloating. Drink up. (But no beer. One beer can lower your heat tolerance for as long as three

days.) Any thirst should be slaked immediately—and preferably with plain unadulterated water.

The biggest myth of all, as has been amply demonstrated, is that anybody engaging in strenuous exercise must—in order to turn in a peak performance—stoke up before participating. It is also probable that the athlete who eats more with the intent of becoming stronger and playing better only becomes fatter, develops excessive eating habits, and stimulates fat cells to multiply and enlarge.

To paraphrase an old maxim: He travels fastest who travels lightest.

What about "the strenuous life" during a fast for the non-athlete and the person not in peak physical condition?

As you might imagine, I cannot agree with the contention, voiced especially by fasting spa operators, that fasting should be a time of complete physical rest even for the healthy person. I have discovered no reason why the healthy person who is fasting for a few days shouldn't continue with the type of exercise to which he or she is *accustomed. Failure to exercise, in fact, brings on fatigue.* Exercise slows down the activity of the pancreas and this prevents a lowering of the sugar level and avoids fatigue.

Dr. Otto Buchinger, who directed tens of thousands of fasts, observed that "we do not conserve any energy by mollycoddling our powers. It simply is not true that exercise impedes rather than enhances weight loss during a fast or that one loses more weight by resting than by being active. Instead of losing fat, the immobile body mainly loses valuable muscle and organic albumen."

But do only as much as you can comfortably do. Avoid doing anything to the point of exhaustion, of course—always good counsel.

If you don't usually exercise, the fasting period would be a good time to get into the habit of walking. You can accomplish a lot of walking during hours otherwise spent preparing food and eating. I insist

those people who fast under my supervision walk briskly for at least one hour every day of a short fast and
at least three hours every day of a long fast. I break
the fast of anyone who can't or won't.

10.

The Contemplative Life

All fasting is . . . a yearning of the soul to merge in the divine essence.

—Mahatma Gandhi

In the quest for serenity and wisdom and heightened states of awareness, fasting has been a revered discipline. Its origins go back millennia, to the Eastern mystics and to the prophets of the Old Testament. It was popular with the savants of ancient Greece and Rome and of the Renaissance. "If practiced with the right intention, it makes man a friend of God," said Tertullian, the Roman theologian. "The demons are aware of that."

To gain mental and spiritual rewards, the membership of the Self-Realization Fellowship* fasts in accordance with the teachings of its guru-founder, Paramahansa Yogananda. In his "bible," *Man's Eternal Quest,* the rewards of fasting are delineated:

1. The spirit within becomes disassociated from the demands of the body as the body itself is freed from gross habits.
2. Fasting gives rest to the overworked organs, the bodily engines.
3. Fasting gives rest to the life force itself, relieving it of extra work. The life force is the sustainer of the body, and through fasting it becomes self-supporting and independent.
4. Overeating every day of the year creates many kinds of disease.

---

*The Fellowship was founded in the United States nearly six decades ago to create understanding among the religions of East and West.

5. Undeviating regularity in eating, whether the system needs food or not, is a curse to the body. The more you concentrate on the palate, the more disease you will have. To enjoy food is fine, but to be a slave of it is the bane of life.

6. The physical effects of fasting are remarkable. A fast of three days on orange juice* will repair the body temporarily, but a long fast will completely overhaul it. (Persons in good health should experience no difficulty in fasting for three days; longer fasts should be undertaken only under experienced supervision. Anyone suffering from a chronic ailment or an organic defect should fast only upon the advice of a physician experienced in fasting procedures.) Your body will feel as strong as steel. But if you want a permanent overhaul you must at all times watch what and how much food you take into your body. There is a great metaphysical science behind fasting. Jesus reminded us of this truth when He said, "Man shall not live by bread alone. . . ." Two things keep you bound to Earth: breath and bread. In sleep, however, you are peacefully unaware of the need for either breath or food; your spirit is detached from body consciousness. Fasting uplifts the mind in the same way.

7. Fasting lets the mind depend on its own power. The mind tells itself: "The solids on which the body used to depend are nothing more than gross condensations of energy. You are pure energy. And you are pure consciousness."

8. The mind, in learning to depend on itself through fasting, can do anything: conquer disease, create prosperity, or realize the supreme goal of life—finding God.

Tennessee Williams, in his autobiography, *Memoirs*, recalls being stranded as a young man in a remote desert area of California. He had neither food nor money to buy food. After the third day of his involuntary fast, he observed "with considerable astonishment" that he no longer felt hungry. "The stomach contracts, the gastric spasms subside and God or some-

*I believe juice with all its calories and tea or soda or coffee should *not* be consumed during a fast. A water-only diet is the true fast and is what I recommend for purest results.—A.C.

body drops in on you invisibly and painlessly injects you with sedation so that you find yourself drifting into a curiously and absolutely inexplicably peaceful condition, and this condition is ideal for meditation on things past and passing and to come, in just that sequence."

11.

The More Beautiful People

Before appearing on a television series to discuss "the ultimate diet," Hugh Downs told me he fasts every Monday to control his weight. He got the idea while visiting Lion Country Safari in California. He learned lions in captivity are not fed one day a week because of their conditioning; in the wilds they had been used to going without food occasionally. "While I do not consider myself a lion, gustatory or literary," Mr. Downs remarked, "I share a mammalian evolution with the species and it occurred to me that I, too, might be healthier if I suspended bombarding my stomach with viands one day a week. The dial of my metabolism appears to be set in such a way that I run about eight pounds heavier than I prefer when I eat as comfortably as I like to eat; the alternative is that I can maintain the weight I desire by running slightly hungry always."

By fasting on Mondays, Mr. Downs finds he can eat pretty much what he wants the other six days and maintain desired weight. His appetite is less on the three days following a one-day fast—still another example that fasting regulates or moderates appetite. "Fasting is indeed *not* starving," he observes. "But unfortunately, as I have traveled through various parts of the world for television productions, I have met people who *are* starving. Maybe if we can get better distribution methods and more people doing themselves good by fasting occasionally, the planet will be a pleasanter place."

George Romney, former Presidential candidate, Michigan governor, and president and board chairman of American Motors, fasts at least one period a month. "It is a means of building spiritual strength, and is at the same time good for the body. The funds saved are contributed to my church for use in assisting those in need. Fasting," he adds, "strengthens control over our appetites, thus contributing to self-mastery."

Governor Edmund ("Jerry") Brown, Jr. was 15 pounds overweight when he embarked on a series of fasts. He would fast for 24 hours or 48 hours or sometimes longer. "The fasting idea was spreading around the Governor's office," said Trish Cruskie, a nutritionist in the California Health Department, "the same way it seems to have spread to many other circles in California."

Vidal Sassoon, the internationally renowned hair stylist, fasts for a 36-hour period every month. (He was described by fashion arbiter Eugenia Sheppard as looking 20 years younger than his acknowledged 48.) What harm can there be, he asks sensibly, in skipping four of the 90 meals we usually eat in the course of a month? He says that the monthly fast makes him feel "marvelous, very light, very pure," while giving his liver and digestive system "a great rest. I've found that it brings me great clarity of thinking and stimulates me to all sorts of new ideas for my work." Mr. Sassoon discovered fasting nearly a score of years ago when he was in a state of nervous exhaustion. His friend Kenneth Haigh, the actor, suggested he pack a sweat suit and a copy of Camus' *The Stranger* and hie himself to a health farm for a week of fasting and rest. In his best seller, *A Year of Beauty and Health,* Mr. Sassoon extols the virtues of fasting as the first step in a long-range program to improve health and appearance. "Remember, you are not depriving your body of food. You are rewarding it with rest. Fasting is a way of reaching full potential."

Helen and Scott Nearing are in their mid-seventies and mid-nineties, respectively, and still fast every Sunday. Mrs. Nearing explains that it is "to give the body and the housekeeper (me) an occasional rest and vacation." The Nearings, who pioneered the back-to-the-land movement in the 1930s—hacking out "the good life," first in Vermont and now in Maine—have not seen a doctor in four decades. "If we were to become ill," Mrs. Nearing told me, "we would fast for an extended period."

John Hill, who founded the public relations firm of Hill and Knowlton half a century ago (it is now the largest public relations firm in the world), first fasted as a young man of 21. He describes that first fast of three or four days as being "exceedingly salutary." In middle age he fasted for seven days after a long siege of knee trouble, which, he says, no doctor or specialist had successfully been able to diagnose or treat. The disorder disappeared and never returned. Mr. Hill, still active at 86, fasts on an intermittent basis and finds it "a beneficial practice."

Gwen Davis, the novelist and screenwriter, met some "spectacularly healthy people" while she was visiting Liza Minnelli during the filming of *Lucky Lady* in Guaymas, Mexico. Those denizens of good health told her that fasting was "a wonderful trip" for their body. "As I had spent most of my life trying to give a wonderful trip to my brain," she wrote me, "I thought it was time to give an equal chance to my slightly 'too, too solid flesh.'" At the end of a two-week fast, she said she never looked or felt better. "My skin, my hair, my body tones were all improved. I actually seemed taller." She now fasts every Monday and tries to fast a second day during the week if she does not have obligatory business lunches or dinners every day. "I always feel better when fasting. The big trick for me is not to think about food. At times this is difficult—bean sprouts and crisp bell peppers and sunflower seeds seem sinfully good." Whenever she finishes a major writing project, Ms. Davis likes to go to the desert and fast for five days "to rid myself of the anxiety and tension that has accumulated." When she loses the struggle to keep from smoking, she fasts to cleanse her system of nicotine and to cut down on the habit. "Fasting never interferes with my normal work routine," she says. "When I did a two-week fast in Guaymas, I completed a first draft of *The Aristocrats,* a novel about a movie company on location. I fasted off and on while writing a book of meditations called *How to Survive in Suburbia When Your Heart's in the Himalayas.* It wouldn't surprise me if fasting contributed to the clarity of thought I needed for the meditations."

Douglas Auchincloss, the socialite, told a Fairchild publication he is casual about fasting, preferring to fit it into his schedule so that it does not interfere with social engagements. He finds Sunday "the good day." He loses about two and one-half pounds on a one-day fast. "I find fasting makes me feel better afterwards. It's no hardship at all."

Dr. John C. Lilly, famous for talking to dolphins and whales, reduced his weight from 210 to 143 pounds on his first fast, 38 years ago. At the first sign of gaining weight, he goes on brief, "corrective" fasts. "It is encouraging," he says, "to see this new generation doing its own myth-making in the areas of fasting and food."

12.
The Medical Orthodoxy

If fasting is so wondrous, the question might well be asked, Why aren't more of us in the medical profession championing it?

I am afraid an attitude has developed among some of us that it is impolitic and risky to try new knowledge or any procedure that did not bear the stamp of approval of our colleagues in the profession, especially if it happened to be a controversial procedure. Though fasting has been around for five millennia, it is controversial still.

The observation has been made that "the human brain is not only an organ of thinking but an organ of survival . . . it is made in such a way as to make us accept as truth that which is only advantage." The advantages of closing one's mind to some fundamentally new truth preclude release not only from the burden of learning something new but also from *unlearning* that which is familiar and therefore secure and comfortable.

The primary discoveries of Harvey, Lister, Pasteur, Ehrlich, and many others were vigorously resisted from within the profession. René Laënnec was expelled from his medical society after inventing "the stethoscope"—a sheet of paper rolled into a tube; one end was placed on the patient's chest and the other was applied to the doctor's ear. Some members of the American Medical Association still contest the need for vitamin supplements (as witness the roaring controversy raised by Nobel Prize-winner Linus Pauling's book *Vitamin C and the Common Cold*), minerals, and X-rays.

I find it incongruous that doctors inexperienced in the fast immediately talk about fasting in terms of danger, yet casually prescribe enormous doses of tranquilizers and sleeping pills for periods of many years, as well as antibiotics and other drugs having the potential for unpleasant, sometimes irreversible side effects, addiction, and a high incidence of morbidity. The attitude of aloofness on the part of the medical profession has allowed fasting to drift almost exclusively into the hands of non-medical groups.

Recently, the Associated Press reported that "the diet of affluent Americans able to afford any foods they choose is less nutritious than it was [in the 1960s]. The problem: We are overfed but remain undernourished. As a result, experts say, 10 percent of the population may be anemic and 35 percent overweight."

There is a popular cliché about weight control: "The only way to lose weight and keep the weight off is to have three balanced, nutritious meals a day." But this approach is simply too frustrating for many people who have a weight problem and need the psychological boost of achieving a quick initial weight loss to motivate them to continue the weight-loss program. It also betrays a lack of flexibility and imagination in exploring alternate methods to the regular eating regimen for solving weight problems. The obese "relish" fasting because it is so quick, helpful, and easy; my reluctant colleagues should seriously consider this fact!

There *is* progress to report. Research into fasting is under way at many medical centers, here and abroad. Members of the Academy of Preventive Medicine have begun to fast patients. *The Journal of the American Medical Association* published the opinion that fasting provides the best method of self-discipline needed by the obese—"one that can be repeated with beneficial effect." *The New England Journal of Medicine* has published the view that fasting is "a valid experience for any otherwise healthy person who has failed to relieve the weight problem by every other method."

What interested me most about the prolonged pro-test fast of Gary Gilmore, the Utah prisoner demanding execution, was the reaction of his doctors. When Gilmore was two weeks into the fast and had lost 25 pounds, the doctors attending him said he could continue the fast for another month without difficulty. The prisoner obviously was in the hands of enlightened medical men.

13.

Fasting for Bodily Ills

In my earlier book on fasting, I put major emphasis on weight-reducing benefits. Overweight is the surpassing health problem in the nation, and I felt certain most readers would primarily be interested in learning about the easiest and quickest way to lose unwanted pounds. I therefore restricted myself in *Fasting: The Ultimate Diet* to several paragraphs about fasting for other health gains.

If I can believe the evidence of my eyes and ears, more people are fasting today than I would have guessed, and many of them are fasting therapeutically to stay well and to rid themselves of dis-ease.

Chronic diseases claim a crippling grip on 35-million of us. Fasting does *not* cure chronic diseases or anything else, but it has helped the body to heal itself of more distresses than we may dream.

In the sixteenth century, the illustrious physician Paracelsus called fasting "the greatest remedy." In Sweden thousands of members of the health organization Hälsofrämjandet fast for up to two weeks as a *preventive* measure. Their goal: "The total regeneration and rejuvenation of all functions of the body."

All of us who fast patients have files bulging with testimonials claiming relief from a whole alphabet of complaints ranging from asthma to viruses. Spa literature abounds with case histories of people who are said to have overcome the agonies of psoriasis, acne, peptic ulcers, constipation, hay fever, arthritis, colitis, varicose veins, dermatological diseases, anemia, eye diseases such as iritis and retinitis, rheumatism, gallstones, stress and nervous exhaustion, diseases of the digestive and respiratory organs—and yes, even the common cold.

A woman in Connecticut who is the secretary-treasurer of a factory in Bridgeport fasts to overcome bouts of arthritis. Each year she fasts for two periods, of ten days and five days, having learned, she says, "the subtle but clear language" of her body. Besides getting relief from her arthritis, she finds her skin after the fast "looks opalescent, clean, and clear, and my mind is sharp, my energy levels are tremendous. My body looks beautiful, I truly love myself, and I am once more happy with the entire world."

A Florida executive told me how fasting relieved his prostate problem. "In the 12th day of the fast my urine stream was free and broad for the first time in eight years. On the 21st day I had the first complete emptying of my bladder (no retention) in eight years."

Two colleagues report encouraging results with diabetics. But I cannot be too emphatic in warning that *no diabetic* should undertake a fast except under the closest medical supervision.

I have found a fast of four days to be an effective first step in detecting the origin of food allergies. With the body rid of all reactions from food, a series of direct testings with different foods is initiated to discover which contain the allergens. By introducing only one food at a meal, we can isolate the offending food or foods. Determining food allergies through fasting frequently gives better results than can be achieved by skin-testing.

In the winter of 1976 I was vacationing in Mexico and visited Villa Vegetariana in Cuernavaca. The villa calls itself "Mexico's rejuvenation resort." Besides fasting its guests, the villa offers a regimen of natural organic foods, sunshine, rest, yoga, and exercise. The villa's director, David Stry, speaks of healing rather than curing: "Only a ham can be cured." He has found fasting allows the body to strengthen its forces against many ills.

At the villa I met guests who assured me their maladies, aches, and disorders were being "healed." Before going there, some had given up hope of feeling well. Years of "doctoring," drugs, and surgery had proved ineffectual. Relief from advanced stages of arthritis seemed to be a recurring wonder at the villa. Mrs. O. W., for example, told me she had cortisone injections back home—to no avail—but after three weeks of fasting, followed by a vegetarian diet, she could walk up stairs again, lift her arms, and go to sleep—all free of pain. A 42-year-old asthmatic alternated fasting with small vegetarian meals, and told Mr. Stry that his miseries had finally vanished. A retired commercial airline pilot's serious varicose vein condition all but disappeared after a seven-day fast.

From other hygienic centers come similar reports of dramatic relief from arthritis and asthma after all other forms of treatment had failed.

From Shalimar, a health spa on the Eastern coast of England, Keki R. Sidhwa—its enthusiastic director who has been fasting patients for a quarter of a century—writes me that most of his guests arrive suffering from "acute and chronic diseases of various kinds." He claims the recovery rate through his fasting program is "85 to 90 percent."

More than 2,300 years ago, Hippocrates, "the father of medicine," made this observation: "Everyone has a doctor in him. We just have to help him in his work."

Otto H. F. Buchinger, who supervised tens of thousands of fasts, observed, "Fasting is . . . a royal road to healing for anyone who agrees to take it for the recovery and regeneration of the body."

Permit me once again to emphasize that a therapeutic fast must be under *strict* medical supervision. The fasting procedure is definitely not for everyone (see chapter 15), and individual testimonials mentioned must not be taken as unqualified approval for all who might fast. Every person is adaptable to fasting in a different manner and degree!

14.

Fasting for Mental Ills

Its realization was a long time coming, but the cliché "we are what we eat" is now understood to be as applicable to the state of our mental health as it is to our physical health. The quality of our nutrition indeed affects our behavior, our mood level, and even our sanity.

The necessity of good nutrition for maintenance of physical health was underscored by those who pioneered in the discovery of the vitamin-deficiency diseases and their cures early in the present century. It took another four decades, or until about 1945, for an understanding to develop of the relationship of nutrition to mental health. Around 1945, Dr. Yuri Nicolayev of the Moscow Psychiatric Institute was introducing the revolutionary concept that mental illness, particularly schizophrenia, could be helped through the recuperative powers of fasting and a revised diet.

Dr. Nicolayev, who has fasted more than 10,000 mentally ill patients, reports unusually encouraging results with those patients who had failed to improve on all other treatment programs. Once given up for "hopeless," 65 percent of patients who experience fasting therapy go on to achieve sufficient improvement to live and function outside of the hospital.

At least two out of every hundred persons on our planet suffer from schizophrenia in some degree. As my good friend Dr. Humphry Osmond points out, this dreadful disease knows no national or cultural boundaries and responds to no quarantine or immunization.

We have learned that with the increasing use of drugs in the treatment of mental and emotional disturbances there has been a corresponding increase in the number of patients who become drug-resistant. Other patients may have toxic reactions or develop other complications, some of which may be irreversible. For patients who do not respond to drug treatments, or who respond negatively, fasting is proving to be a valuable alternative.

In 1970 and again in 1972, Dr. Nicolayev invited me to observe in his therapeutic fasting unit and to discuss with him and his large staff my work in orthomolecular treatment. The Moscow Psychiatric Institute consists of a 3,000-bed research center with a staff of 500 physicians. The fasting treatment is conducted in an 88-bed unit.

The fast itself lasts about a month. It is terminated when appetite returns, breath is fresh, the tongue becomes clear, and symptoms are alleviated—signs that a fast of any length should be broken.

After breaking the fast, the patient stays in the hospital an additional number of days equal to the length of the fast. Refeeding begins with a salt-free diet of fruit, vegetables, and some form of acidulated milk. The quantities of food are gradually increased. Meat, eggs, and fish are excluded. Bread is not offered until the sixth or seventh day.

About half of Dr. Nicolayev's patients who were examined after a period of six years had maintained their improved condition. Relapses occurred among those patients who added protein foods from animal sources to the prescribed diet. The maximum effects of the treatment are manifested two or three months after treatment is completed providing the diet has been followed precisely.

One form of schizophrenia prevalent in the U.S.S.R. and whose prognosis had *always* been quite poor responds positively to the fasting treatment. This syndrome is dysmorphobia. It is characterized by delusions of physical shortcomings, and the patient is obsessed by a fear of the escape of offending gases and odors from the body. He or she is convinced that everyone near can hear the sounds and smell the odors. There are usually accompanying convictions of being ugly and undersized and universally repellent. It is impressive that fasting can eradicate even paranoid delusions.

Other types of schizophrenia are alleviated during the fasting and recovery periods. The manic phase of manic-depressive illness can be brought under control in the first week of a fast.

My own experience with treating schizophrenics with fasting was conducted in Gracie Square Hospital in New York City. I made it a prerequisite for admission to the treatment that the subject had been ill with schizophrenia for at least five years and unresponsive to all prior forms of treatment. Another requirement was the consent of the patient and his family. Since the fasting treatment requires the patient's full cooperation, there is no hope of success unless the patient is acutely aware of the gravity of his illness and is willing to give more than passive consent to trying a different approach. I also stipulated that my patients stay out of bed and remain active. They could leave the hospital in the morning and take long walks about the city. (They were free to leave therapy whenever they wished.) They were required to walk, preferably briskly, a minimum of three hours a day. Paradoxically, without three hours of exercise daily, feelings of weakness developed and the fast had to be arbitrarily broken. If a patient willfully broke the fast by eating, treatment was stopped and the patient was discharged from the hospital.

Everyone drank a minimum of two quarts of water every day. If a patient failed—or refused—to drink this amount, I terminated the fast. Daily cleansing enemas and showers or baths were imperative. During the shower or bath, the patient was encouraged to stimulate circulation by using a loofa straw mitt for a washcloth. Patients who had been on medication were able to dispense with it by the end of the first week. Everyone in the program was required to give up smoking—and did.

The fasting period was tolerated surprisingly easily by these very ill people. There were some complications during the recovery period. These occurred mostly from overeating when protein was introduced into the diet. Patients soon learned they had to stick to the prescribed diet in the specified amounts. They had to stop eating before they felt full. In some, the protein addition to the diet produced a period of excitation, tension, or sleeplessness. Sleep medication was prescribed for these patients.

Of the 35 men and women who participated in my fasting project, 24 have not relapsed into illness.

These conclusions can be drawn about treating schizophrenic patients with the controlled fast:

1. While the fast of 25 or more days may lead to some degree of exhaustion, it also serves as a powerful stimulus to subsequent recuperation.

2. Fasting insures rest of the digestive tract, which in itself is a normalizing aid.

3. The acidosis induced by fasting probably plays an important role in neutralizing some of the toxins that may have contributed to the schizophrenic condition.

Schizophrenics have a higher protein level than non-schizophrenic people. Fasting therapy mobilizes the proteins in the body. The process peaks in about seven days. After the fast, the protein level is within normal range. Within three to six months the level tends to rise to the pre-fast level; it is another reason for undergoing recurrent periodic short fasts.

After the publication of *Fasting: The Ultimate Diet,* I heard from the former patient cited as an example of one who had been functioning effectively since completing treatment. He wrote me protesting my use of the word *effectively.* Apparently I had understated his case. "I am very successful in almost everything and happy," he wrote me, "and I think I can appreciate life far more than most people."

Dr. Abe Hoffer, of Saskatoon, Saskatchewan, who has written extensively on mental illness, still wonders why physicians—especially psychiatrists—"are so surprised when they hear of the beneficial effects of a fast. Many become as enraged over the fast as they are when someone mentions megavitamins. I have now seen severe and chronic schizophrenics who had not responded to any previous treatment—including megavitamins, drugs and electro-convulsive treatment—recover after a supervised fast."

What do you eat? is the most neglected question in all of medicine. If more doctors were asking this question and listening sensitively to the answers, the cost of all kinds of illnesses—physical as well as mental—could be reduced.

15.
Who Can Fast—and Who Can't

You should have a thorough physical examination before commencing any fast, even if you feel and look in the best of health. Without such an examination, it is impossible to determine what's going on in the body.

No matter how well you are, you may have some "silent" condition or ailment that would be aggravated by fasting. The blood tests done before the fast serve as a base line from which one monitors the changes occurring during and after the fast.

There are many people who should never fast, and others who should fast only under the closest supervision. You must not fast if you have any of these conditions: heart diseases, especially a predisposition to thrombosis, tumors, bleeding ulcers, cancer, blood diseases, active pulmonary diseases, diabetes (juvenile), gout, liver diseases, kidney diseases, recent myocardial infarction, cerebral diseases.

Any condition requiring long-term use of medication also rules out fasting.

A very thin person can fast, but not for a longer time than one day in a month.

A pregnant woman must not fast, not even for one day. While she herself might tolerate the fast quite well, the developing brain of the fetus might suffer irreparable damage.

A new mother must not fast until her obstetrician has examined her and found that the uterus is back to the pre-pregnant state. For most women this can take more than a month. While nursing, a woman should not fast.

It is perfectly safe for older people to fast, but no older person should *start* fasting without his doctor's approval. There are many elderly people who have been fasting all their lives, and there is considerable evidence that fasting may contribute to a longer life. On the tenth day of a fast, Gandhi at age sixty-four was said to have the constitution of a man of forty. Good-health advocate Bernarr Macfadden discovered fasting in his youth and made it a permanent part of his exceedingly long life. The novelist Upton Sinclair, who lived to be a nonagenarian, found in fasting "a perfect health, a new state of existence, a feeling of purity and happiness," and said that it enabled him to "overwork with impunity." Hygienist and outdoorsman Paul Bragg fasted into his mid-nineties—and was still hiking up and down mountains.

I don't approve of children fasting. It is not known what effect fasting can have on a child's growth processes, and no one should undergo a long fast during years of growth. (I am asked if fasting can help in the treatment of children with learning disabilities. What may help *these* children is a radical change of diet. "Offending foods" make children hyperactive or aggravate hyperactivity caused by something else. In adults they cause fatigue and depression. The elimination of cane sugar and food additives—such as artificial colorings and flavorings and preservatives—helps many children to achieve and learn.)

Among people who *can* fast with great benefit are those with high blood pressure and high cholesterol levels. Abstaining from food can often reduce these readings to normal range. Proper dietary changes can maintain the lowered levels.

High blood pressure should drop progressively during a longer fast. It should remain lower if the weight is kept off. There is a relationship between diabetes and overweight, high blood pressure and high cholesterol. By whatever means weight is lost, lowered blood pressure is the accompanying blessing. By the way, quick weight loss with its correspondingly sudden reduction in blood pressure can bring on feelings of dizziness. Some of these sensations can be averted by avoiding sudden changes in the posture of the body. Rise slowly from a sitting position. Sit up slowly from a lying position. Crouch rather than bend when you pick up something from the floor.

On a longer fast there is a temporary elevation of the cholesterol level. The explanation is that cholesterol deposits "shake loose" and augment the measurable level. But this "increase" is not real; in fact, fasting brings down the level.

Within a week to ten days after the longer fast, the cholesterol level drops to a point much below the prefast level. (The same desirable result is observed when there is loss of weight by any means.) During a long fast, the body chemistry undergoes many beneficial changes. The report one hears about fasting raising cholesterol levels is another of those quarter-truths used by the biased to frighten someone out of undertaking a fast.

There are signs that indicate a fast should be prematurely broken. They usually occur when metabolism is not functioning properly. Persistence of hunger beyond the fourth day, the unexpected return of appetite, persistent irregularity of heartbeat, intestinal spasms, and sustained headaches, vomiting spells, nausea, and dizziness are indications that the fast should be broken and the refeeding program begun. These manifestations are experienced by a small minority of the people who fast.

Hypoglycemics are particularly sensitive to the fasting process on the first day. Blood sugar may drop, and there could be symptoms of weakness, anxiety, and fatigue. If such feelings persist into a second or third day, it would be wise to terminate the fast. Hypoglycemics should fast only under a doctor's *daily* supervison. (Anyone under a doctor's care for any reason should *not* fast, *for even one day,* without approval.)

To repeat: the person in average good health can fast safely for four weeks or longer, but should keep in touch with his or her doctor daily. The long fast must always be a hospital procedure.

16.

Hope for the Young

A herd of mountain sheep in the Canadian province of Alberta is in danger of being killed off by junk food distributed by tourists. The herd eats the candy and other junk food proffered and neglects the normal grass diet. The animals lose weight, and wardens fear females are not producing enough high-quality milk.

Children are fed baby foods spiked with sugar right after they are weaned. They are also fed lollipops and gumdrops by their mothers, fathers, grandparents, their pediatricians, and, so help me, their dentists. Sugar in one form or another is omnipresent in their diet. Little wonder so many of them develop behavioral difficulties, become hyperactive and malnourished, and lack interest in their studies. (The Confectioners Association gave an award to a prominent professor of nutrition for his books and other writings suggesting we'd be better off if we ate *more* sugar and arguing there was nothing wrong with food additives.)

How quickly—and, alas, inevitably—our kids join the fast-food generation! From the moment they get out of bed in the morning, they are besieged on all sides by messages urging them to eat mal-nourishing food. Do they ever hear about the good taste and nutritive values of carrots and sunflower seeds and roasted soybeans? Joan Gussow of Columbia University rightly asks if it is moral to allow our children to be assaulted "with a barrage of food products that add up to audio-visual diabetes." It is distressing to note that the children of the house may be subjected to the nutritional rot of sugar, soft drinks and candy bars and

TV dinners while only the dog of the house rates a balanced diet containing all the essential nutrients.

But there is cheering evidence that a corner is being turned. An encouraging number of young people seem to be acquiring exemplary dietary habits and rejecting the foods hawked to them so persistently in print and electronic advertisements.

In his widely syndicated newspaper column, Sydney J. Harris wrote he wouldn't be surprised if *his* children knew more about nutrition than most doctors do. He said they've studied the subject seriously and have taken vitamin and mineral supplements for years. "The empirical results," he wrote, "are a flowing testimony to their health, strength and endurance."

This knowledge and concern about good eating habits—and I'm sorry to have to concur—does not owe as much as it should to the medical profession, which Mr. Harris points out "is happily writing out millions of prescriptions a month for conditions that would not have existed if proper nutrition had been attended to in the first place."

During a trip West I saw some encouraging evidence of commendable nutritional programs for the young.

President John Howard of Lewis and Clark College in Portland, who believes the healthy mind needs the support of a healthy body, was concerned the students were being fed a faulty diet. He took action. He ordered a dramatic about-face in the bill of fare. The institutional feeding company servicing the college was told it must develop alternate menus emphasizing natural and nutritious foods.

Among the innovations were buckwheat groats, chop suey made with soybean sprouts, yogurt, vegetable "steaks," granola, toasted wheat germ, cooked whole grains, and fruits and vegetables assembled in tantalizing presentations. Sweet, fatty, highly processed foods were phased out of the students' diet while the nutritional replacements were introduced one at a time so that the switch would not be abrupt. "If I hadn't been told something was up," remarked one student, "I'm not sure I would have noticed the change—except the chow was tasting better and better."

The University of California campus at Santa Cruz developed a student garden project dedicated to organic, ecological horticulture. A young woman, Linda Wilshusen, who is a recent graduate of that college, told me the project was designed to "celebrate and foster a true and clear sense of the interdependence of man and his natural environment." She recalled the students ate the food grown in the garden, and that the Whole Earth Restaurant on campus featured such enticing items as pumpkin mushroom soup, lemon-bean salad, brown rice burgers, fresh carrot cake, wheat germ muffins, nut loafs, millet porridge, caraway cabbage salad, whole wheat pasta, and persimmon pudding.

From the other side of the continent comes equally good news. The Board of Education of the State of West Virginia unanimously voted a ban on the sale in all public schools of candy, chewing gum, soft drinks, and flavored ice bars. A member of the board said that while it was trying to teach students the value of good nutrition, "there was still available in vending machines food that was bad for them." For those school districts dependent on the profits from vending machines, a list of foods acceptable for vending was compiled. The food included milk, fruit juices, soups, fresh fruits, raisins, peanuts, and yogurt. (As long ago as 1950 this nutritionally progressive state levied a tax on all soft drinks. The money went toward financing West Virginia's University Medical Center in Morgantown.)

The quality of the cuisine began to improve immediately, according to *Prevention* magazine, when innovative Franconia College in New Hampshire discharged its professional catering company and students took over in the cafeteria. (The move to student direction was originally in the interest of cutting expenses.) The students substituted fresh foods for frozen and dried and instant foods. They eliminated white bread and used whole grain bread bought from a local bakery. Yogurt, honey and granola became staples. The soda-vending machine was removed and a soft-drink known as "bug juice" was struck from the menu. By eating better, the students found they were also spending less.

In the Westchester County (New York) town of Hartsdale, a volunteer group of 12 enlightened parents was given authority by the school board to supervise the choice of food served to the 3,500 children in district schools. Eliminated from menus was every food containing artificial colors, flavors and preservatives. The parents substituted whole wheat bread for white bread, decreased the amount of sugar used in recipes, introduced hard-boiled eggs, raisins, sunflower seeds, and a locally baked brand of cookies free of artificial substances. "We are not crazy health food faddists," explained one of the Hartsdale parents. "But it is no more difficult for the vendor to serve nutritious food than overly processed, artificially colored food. Caterers who need our business can be taught to change their ways."

Nutrition is scheduled to be taught from kindergarten through the sixth grade in Hartsdale. A curriculum incorporating the new knowledge about food and its consequences is in the planning stage. Students will learn that orange juice comes from a round, orange-colored fruit and that milk comes from a live cow—not from cartons in a supermarket.

Many of these students may be able to teach the so-called "specialists" a thing or two. Not long ago a university professor of nutrition declared in a press interview that additives were not only *thought* to be safe, but *were* safe—"absolutely. No ifs, ands, or buts." Within a month of the interview, the Food and Drug Administration announced it was moving to ban all further use of the widely applied Red No. 2 on the grounds that it had been shown to cause cancer in laboratory animals.

Good nutritional practices are getting youngsters off to a good start in Allentown, Pennsylvania. The day-care center there run by Volunteers of America has been serving meals of cashew-millet casseroles, brown rice and spinach casseroles, soybean "surprise," and broiled liver. The kids love them. Some of these three-to-five-year-olds come back for seconds and thirds on the liver, which they call "steak." They are also served fresh fruit, mixed raw nuts, seeds, dried fruits, fruited gelatin with yogurt, and homemade whole grain bread. Homemade and natural foods, the Volunteers learned, also cost less than canned and processed foods.

At Bell Top School in North Greenbush, New York, near Albany, candy canes and gumdrops were notably absent from a Christmas party. "The children were not disappointed, they were delighted," reported *Prevention* magazine. "The children had voted unanimously to have only natural goodies that would taste good now and not hurt them later."

Among the hardest misconceptions to quash is the one that eating habits can't be changed or relearned. We have seen that young people's eating preferences *can* be reoriented. A few generations ago, we ate mostly unprocessed or lightly processed foods and we ate at home. More of our food is now industrially prepared and much of it is consumed away from home—and on the run. The consumer advocate Bess Myerson passes along the fact that 80 percent of vending machine sales, which total $6-billion annually, are in junk food categories.

The omens seem favorable that we might be able to re-educate ourselves to the good nutrition—and to the good taste—of our grandparents. It will probably be our children who will lead the way. Already many of them understand that just because it's advertised it is not necessarily good for anyone except the money-oriented processor.

A story in *Fairpress,* a weekly published for residents of Fairfield County, Connecticut, sums up the potential. "Oily French fries, greasy potato chips, filler-packed hot dogs [which contain bone dust and "allowable amounts" of bone splinters]: they're favorites at the beach . . . or are they? Although no one is about to launch a campaign for natural foods to be sold at local public beaches, many people would buy such wholesome items as fresh fruit and fruit juice if they were offered."

At The Door in Manhattan, a "center of alternatives" for troubled youngsters, the kids have crossed out the sign "Candy Shoppe" on the vending machine and written in its place "Food for Thought." Five nights a week some 100 kids dine there on whole and natural foods, which they say have killed their taste for vended junk.

With intelligent eating habits learned early, there would be much less need later for diets—for even "the ultimate diet"—to combat overweight and related ailments.

We will get the food we demand. A nutritionally enlightened public can bring about a revolution in the food industry that can only contribute to the public health.

17.
Sharing and Protesting

Fasting also has altruistic applications.

In effect, the mass fast day can focus concentration on the inequities of food distribution throughout the world—and on a way of alleviating them in some small measure.

Fast days for just such purposes are now organized and nationwide—and increasingly popular. The Thursday before Thanksgiving is taking on the aura of a national holiday. On that day, about a million of us treat our digestive systems to a rest and give the money we would have spent on food for ourselves to support projects that help people in Africa, Asia, and Latin America grow food.

This annual national fast day is sponsored by Oxfam-America, a Boston-headquartered organization dedicated to reminding "thoughtful people of the deepening world food crisis." Pope Paul describes the situation of hunger in the world as "a crisis of solidarity and civilization." The opportunity to convert one day of "hunger" into practical aid for the famished has been hailed as an alternative to inaction, helplessness, and apathy. It is a day of hope.

(And fasting to call attention to the world's hungry is worlds safer than parachuting off the 110-story north tower of the World Trade Center in New York. Which is what Owen Quinn did in 1975. He now confines his appeal to the lecture circuit and leaves the tower to King Kong.)

Oxfam fasts are organized by local educational, religious, civic, and charitable agencies and by individuals. Interest in the event has been stimulated by the participation of such well-known figures as Dr. Benjamin Spock, Senator Richard Clark (of Iowa), Harvard President Derek Bok, the inexhaustible Dick Gregory, and Frances Lappé, the author of *Diet for a Small Planet*. Wisconsinites have been invited to participate by their governor, Patrick Lucy. He proclaimed the fasting day "a chance for us to make a small, personal and significant contribution."

Typical of the enthusiastic responses to national fast days are these comments which Oxfam has shared with us:

"Thank you for providing the structure by which we were able to respond to the world food crisis. . . . The fast focused student attention on this aspect of life with which they were unfamiliar. . . . Thank you for attempting to make us think: think of our bodies, think of our priorities. Thank you for helping me to awaken myself and the people I work with. . . . Everyone in the class who fasted made it through the whole day without eating. It wasn't too difficult and we knew we were not starving. Still, it made us understand a little better what hunger is. . . . If the need for sharing and caring were brought down to a personal level of responsibility all-year-through, we might begin to live more appreciatively by sharing our abundance which rightly belongs to everyone everywhere. . . . We were going out for a pizza when we read about the fast, so we skipped the pizza. Here's the money. . . . We held a foodless food sale and raised $100—the bottles of water went like hotcakes."

Oxfam's Fast for a World Harvest inspired suggestions that such fasts be increased to a once-a-month or even a once-a-week basis.

Between Christmas and New Year's at the end of 1975, Dick Gregory led a week-long fast calling attention to the food shortage in America and in the poor countries of the world. About 120 people joined him at Dr. Ralph Abernathy's Baptist Church in Atlanta. This fast of social protest was endorsed by Stevie Wonder, John Lennon, Eugene McCarthy, Muhammad Ali, Barbra Streisand, and César Chavez. Many people simply can't afford to eat any more, Mr. Gregory contended, pointing out how some have had to take to shoplifting and some to eating dog food. He put forward two proposals: that a new Cabinet post—Secretary of Food and Nutrition—be created and that a new kind of food stamp be issued to guarantee staples like rice, beans, and corn at ten cents a pound.

The prophet Muhammad noted that "the hunger Muslims experience while fasting also enables them to appreciate the hunger of the poor and the needy." Dr. Ahmad H. Sakr, writing in the *Journal of the American Dietetic Association,* suggests that partial fasting could be of some help to politicians "concerned with curbing inflation and energy crises, since people should be able to consume less food and the extra food could be given to those in need. Also, people would have extra time for work, and productivity might be increased."

The individual fast is also employed as an instrument of persuasion. Mahatma Gandhi was the founder in modern times of the protest fast; his inspiring example is being emulated to the present day everywhere in the world.

For example, in righteous indignation over America's underground nuclear tests, a retired professor of ethics, Ichiro Moritaki, has fasted off and on for twenty years before the Cenotaph, the Hiroshima monument containing the names of those killed by the atomic bomb. In the Philippines, a senator, Benigno Aquino, fasted to call attention to the "repressiveness" of the dictatorship of President Marcos. Many individuals fast to protest Soviet repressions.

Commonplace in the United States are hunger strikes in prisons where the inmates are striving to bring about any number of reforms, not the least of which is the deplorable state of the prison diet.

Without for a moment denigrating the aims of Oxfam

and similar organizations and dedicated individuals, the point must be underscored that people who fast to help others and to protest political and social issues are helping themselves at the same time. Any fast is self-serving. One feels better physically as well as mentally, and in the Oxfam context one is entitled to that extra boost in self-regard for "sacrificing" to serve the needs of others.

18.

Fasting Vacations: Retreats and Traveling

One of the laudable fashions of the seventies is the health-improvement vacation.

More and more people are spending vigorous holidays playing tennis, surfing, cross-country skiing, scuba diving, hiking, cycling, mountain climbing, and shooting river rapids.

Others—no less conscientious about their health—are electing to find the true rest and renewal fasting can bring. These people are seeking retreats where fasting and related practices are featured.

A criterion for a fast of any length away from home is the scope of activities available. The more facilities there are, the more involvement, the more quickly time passes, of course.

The best place for a long fast is a spa with facilities for blood analyses, X-rays, electrocardiograms—in other words, a place where examinations are given and the fast is conducted under daily supervision and guidance.

A hospital is the ideal setting for the obese or the seriously ill to fast. Reasonably healthy people should not go to hospitals or to those retreats whose principal concern is in treating serious sickness.

People in good health should avoid the spa where lying in bed is encouraged and where exercise is not part of the daily program. For healthy people, the fasting process is enhanced by exercise.

In my previous book I gave brief descriptions of

several places here and abroad where fasting is conducted. Since then I've learned about other such places. This information is offered with the reminder that mention of any retreat in these pages does not constitute any endorsement or recommendation.

New Age Health Farm. This picturesque haven in the Catskills, 100 miles northwest of New York City, is approached via a long maple-flanked driveway which winds past a swimming pool and through fields of rolling grasslands. Poised against the backdrop of fields and mountains is a cluster of white Colonial buildings. The farm occupies 106 lush acres (50 of which are forested) at an elevation of 1,800 feet. It is conveniently situated for a penitential stopover after a gluttonous visit to Grossinger's, nine miles down the road.

The main disciplines are fasting—either the water fast or the juice fast*—and yoga.

Enemas are prescribed for everyone fasting a week or longer. They are regarded here as deterrents to headaches, nausea, or dizzy spells, and they are held to promote greater losses of weight.

There is a daily program of nature walks, Hatha Yoga, swimming in season, and working in the vegetable garden. Tobogganing, skiing, and horseback-riding facilities are available in the area. In the evening, after a candle-lit "dinner" of water or fruit juice, there is usually a lecture or group discussion on some aspect of healthful living. There are private or group consultations for airing emotional problems and stimulating spiritual awareness.

The farm accommodates 70 people, and all rooms have private baths. The owners, Elza and Graeme Graydon, request that children and pets be left at home.

ADDRESS: New Age Health Farm, Neversink, New York, 12765.

---

*Again, I recommend only the water fast.

The Shangri-La. This natural hygiene retreat with 66 guest rooms is set among groves and gardens four miles from the Gulf of Mexico. Founded in 1961, it is dedicated to a program of "health education and better understanding of the ecological requirements of man."

A creek meanders through the 10-acre resort. Among the recreational facilities are tennis courts, a jogging track, a swimming pool, a Ping-Pong pavilion, a shuffleboard court, and a horseshoe pit. Shangri-La provides twice-daily bus service to nearby beaches.

The resort attracts therapeutic fasters of all ages, but the majority are more than 40 years of age. Shangri-La is not a medical institution, but physicians may be called in at a guest's request.

Only distilled water is served during the fast. The fast is broken with freshly squeezed juice or whole fruit. Recommended for the postfast program are fresh fruits, vegetables, nuts taken raw, and an adherence to the basic principles of natural hygiene. Sunbathing —preferably in the nude—and exercising are encouraged. There are daily exercise classes and separate solaria for men and women.

At least three nights a week there are lectures on all phases of hygienic living. The managing director is R. J. Cheatham.

ADDRESS: The Shangri-La, Bonita Springs, Florida, 33923.

Dr. Acers-Vita-Dell Spa. Elva S. Acers, D.C., the founder, heartily concurs with the contentions of the late Dr. Alexis Carrel, the Nobel Prize-winning geneticist, that fasting purifies and profoundly modifies our tissues and that it is toxic waste accumulation—and not years—that accelerates the aging process and death itself. Fasting here is viewed as "a fantastic rest for the entire body."

A typical day at Vita-Dell begins at 6:00 A.M. with a walk in the desert, exercise, and a swim in the mineral-water pool. Then, rest and the daily care. Then, more rest, walks, and a swim.

The program of each guest is tailored to fit his or her needs. Post-fast diets are also fashioned on an individual basis, but there's a high percentage of raw foods. The length of the fast is also individually determined.

"The fasting approach to weight loss is fantastic," the director notes. "It is beneficial in all areas and aids the entire body to normalizing and regaining a natural, healthful, balanced function. It helps relieve the patient of a perverted appetite for tobacco, sweets, and junk foods."

Dr. Acers recommends at least a two-week stay to allow from seven to eleven days for fasting and ample time for breaking the fast.

ADDRESS: Dr. Acers-Vita-Dell Spa, 13 495 Palm Drive, Desert Hot Springs, California, 92240.

Hippocrates Health Institute. This nonprofit organization was founded a quarter of a century ago by Ann Wigmore, D.D., N.D., who is still its director. It is dedicated to Hippocrates, who said, "Let living foods be thy medicine."

One of the aims of the institute is to teach country living in the city. The ground floor has a garden area and a sprouting room. On the second floor is a stoveless kitchen, which dispenses only natural foods in an uncooked state. Fruits and vegetables predominate over starches and proteins, and students learn to combine foods properly. A massage room is on the third floor, and sleeping accommodations are on the upper floors.

ADDRESS: Hippocrates Health Institute, 25 Exeter Street, Boston, Massachusetts, 02116.

New Image. Canada's first major fasting facility occupies a manor two blocks from Lake Ontario in one of Toronto's pleasantest residential areas. The clientele are women with weight problems.

The regimen for a one-week program includes individual counseling on weight control and group therapy conducted by a psychologist. There are evening lectures on subjects pertaining to good health and good eating habits.

The week of fasting in residence is followed by eight sessions intended to help keep the "new image" intact.

ADDRESS: New Image, 1867 Yonge Street, Suite 600, Toronto MAS 1Y5, Canada.

The Place. Eight miles from San Salvador, El Salvador's capital, and 2,000 feet above sea level with commanding views of lakes and forested hills. The Place offers pure mountain air, year-round sunbathing and swimming, corrective exercises, and body building —"an atmosphere designed to induce rest and recuperation from nervous tension."

The director is Dr. Carlos Rosendo Arguello, a natural hygienist who claims he has supervised 30,000 fasts—5,000 were more than a month in length. He prefers to have guests who are "conscious that true health cannot be bought but built through a natural way of life."

Each room has a private bath, and guests should plan to stay at least a week. Shopping trips and visits to nearby archeological sites can be arranged.

After breaking the fast, guests are offered balanced meals with organically grown fruits and vegetables.

Dr. Arguello has published extensively on health subjects.

ADDRESS: The Place, Apartado 2199, San Salvador, El Salvador, Central America.

Instituto Dietético Diquecito. Situated in a peaceful picturesque valley near Argentina's second city, Córdoba, and downstream from a large reservoir, the institute looks like an Alpine chalet. The building is three stories high and has 43 rooms facing the surrounding hills. The founder, Dr. P. Busse Grawitz, asserts that the institute is the only one of European styling in South America and people of "elevated status" make frequent use of it. "Fasting cures" have been in effect here for 31 years.

Diquecito has a laboratory, a nursing staff, and a kitchen. Each patient is given a complete health examination. A goal is "liquidation" of chronic pains, especially rheumatism. Diet is tailored to each person's needs.

Additional facilities are a large dining room, a large recreation hall for games and music and lectures, and a swimming pool. Visitors are encouraged to do a lot of walking and to hike up and down the hill paths, but are cautioned against extreme physical exertion.

Dr. Busse Grawitz tries to have a personal talk daily with each guest.

ADDRESS: Instituto Dietético Diquecito, at Diquecito, 5151 La Calera, Provincia de Córdoba, Argentina.

Shrubland Hall Health Clinic. Patients at tranquil and well-accoutred Shrubland are generally encouraged to begin their stay with a three-day fast of lemon and water.

Shrubland will fast a patient for only five days in any one week. The average weight loss on this regimen is usually 10 pounds per woman, 14 pounds per man. Patients fasting solely for health reasons are found to have the most positive approach to fasting.

Shrubland was built 236 years ago and was completely modernized recently. It is England's only clinic run by its owners and the only one with two physicians in residence. Patients are thoroughly examined on arrival and periodically during their stay.

Shrubland is a 75-minute train ride from London and is practically self-sufficient. An organic garden provides fruits and vegetables. Dairy products come from the clinic's own herd. Every day (for those not fasting) there is fresh bread baked from homegrown wheat and barley. Drinking water is drawn from a well.

Treatments available are massages, saunas, sitz and herbal and peat baths, physioelectric therapy, spot reducing, facials, waxings, manicures, chiropody, and hairdressing.

Exercise classes based on Hatha Yoga are held

in the gym. Facilities include a swimming pool, gymnasium, solarium, billiard room, and library. Patients are urged to take long walks.

The sixth Baron de Saumarez is a co-director with his wife, Lady Julia de Saumarez, a trained dietician. Her preference is for "the original nature-cure diet"—twice as much fruit and vegetables as protein and carbohydrates.

ADDRESS: Shrubland Hall Health Clinic, Coddenham, Suffolk, IP6 9QH, England.

The Tyringham Clinic. A former private Georgian mansion, designed by Sir John Soane, this 100-room naturopathic clinic is situated about halfway between London and Birmingham amidst 30 acres of woodlands and landscaped organic gardens. Operating as a non-profit charity, it is an eclectic center of natural healing catering annually to 2,000 chronically sick patients.

"One of the main causes of illness is wrong eating," asserts the director, Sidney Rose-Neil. "The mystery is not why do we get ill, but how do we remain well for so long." The philosophy here: "Man has the natural right to be healthy throughout a long and happy life."

Besides fasting, treatment includes acupuncture ("to promote tissue repair and enhance a sense of well being"; balneotherapy (mineral baths); breathing exercises (to increase the supply of oxygen to the body); hydrotherapy (sitz and steam baths); massages; herbal, homeopathic, and vitamin medications; osteopathy; physiotherapy involving ultraviolet and infra-red radiation; traction; sauna; seaweed and wax baths; oatmeal baths (for skin complaints); inhalation of herbs and peat packs; psychocounseling; relaxation techniques; gymnasium exercises; and yoga. All types of chronic illnesses except infectious diseases and terminal cases are treated.

At Tyringham "health is harmony: physical, emotional, and spiritual. Man is more than the sum total of his parts, more than just chemicals. We are part of the cosmos and we cannot separate ourselves from it." A "wonderful feeling of timelessness" envelops the patient here. Fasting's physiologic and cleansing attributes are considered more vital here than weight reduction.

There are facilities for tennis, bowling, miniature golf, badminton, croquet, two swimming pools, and a library.

Fees are determined by operational costs and accommodations, and are adjusted to ability to pay.

ADDRESS: The Tyringham Clinic, Newport Pagnell, Bucks MK 16 9 ER, England.

Shalimar. Named after the legendary Mogul gardens of India, Shalimar is a mansion in tranquil English surroundings, a 10-minute walk from the Channel. The director, Keki R. Sidhwa, a naturopath-osteopath, has been described as "a human dynamo;" he runs 30 miles every week. He is editor of the *Hygienist* and president of the British Natural Hygiene Society. Today, at the age of 50, Mr. Sidhwa is in vigorous good health.

Shalimar, which means "abode of health, beauty, and peace," caters to both the sick and the well in a natural approach to healthful living. Mr. Sidhwa says, "If you are feeling tired and listless and have a cold, ache or fever, do what the animals do instinctively: fast." Rest—physical, mental, sensory—is urged; the fast is followed by a vegan or vegetarian diet based strongly on compost-grown fruits and vegetables.

Management's attitude is no nonsense, no pampering. There are none of the accoutrements and facilities found in a luxury retreat.

Exercise (yoga) and siestas are on the order of the day. Guests are taught that man cannot live healthily by diet alone or by exercise alone or by rest alone or by fasting alone, but only by "the judicious application of all the elements, both physiological and psychological, that are needed for life and living."

Mr. Sidhwa says, "Shalimar has had excellent success with lowering blood pressure and cholesterol readings. The readings tend to drop during the fast, and remain at a lower level if the person eats hygienically. We have also learned the surest way to break alcohol and smoking habits is the 20- to 30-day fast."

ADDRESS: Shalimar, First Avenue, Frinton-on-Sea, Essex CO 13 9E7, England.

Here is a reprise of some of the spas described in *Fasting: The Ultimate Diet:*

The Bay'n Gulf Health Resort, 18207 Gulf Boulevard, Redington Shores, Florida, 33708. Manager, Dorothy K. Brosious. Set 300 yards from the Gulf of Mexico, it has easy access to white sandy beaches and swimming. "The road to health" followed for weight reduction and maintenance begins with a fast and progresses to a diet of fresh fruits, fresh vegetables, nuts, and seeds. The proclaimed goal here: harmony between body and nature. The clientele, mostly women, is told "fasting is the best and safest way to lose extra poundage."

Esser's Hygienic Rest Ranch, P.O. Box 161, Lake Worth, Florida, 33460. Director, William Esser. Facilities: tennis, volleyball, hiking, biking, weight-lifting. After the fast, guests are given organic fruits and vegetables, mostly grown at the ranch. Mr. Esser has supervised more than 15,000 fasts.

Pawling Health Manor, P.O. Box 401, Hyde Park, New York, 12538. Director, Robert Gross. Set in the patrician Hudson River estate country, 100 miles north of New York City, this converted manor house with a motel-like annex plays host principally to a clientele interested in weight reduction. Other than evening lectures on diet, there is no programmed activity. Guests are free to take day trips to interesting historic sites in the area.

Buchinger-Klinik am Bodensee, 777 Überlingen, Lake Constance, West Germany; *Clinica Buchinger,* Marbella, S.A., Marbella (Málaga), Spain. Manager, H. Ph. Wilhelmi. In these attractive, well-appointed

West European spas, fasting is supplemented by hydrotherapy, massages, and gymnastic exercises. There is constant medical supervision; an initial physical examination is obligatory. Mr. Wilhelmi holds that conscientious fasters will be rewarded with nothing short of a new concept of themselves and the potential that life offers them. He coined the phrase "incinerator action" to describe how the body, while fasting, rids itself of waste products.

Villa Vegetariana, P.O. Box 1228, Cuernavaca, Mexico. Proprietor, David Stry. Altitude: 5,000 feet. Facilities include a ceramic-tiled swimming pool, gymnasium, hammocks, swings, and private solaria for nude sunbathing. Management now accepts guests with no previous fasting experience.

Fasting and traveling vacations should be compatible, though you rarely see them keeping company. Travel is usually equated with the discovery of new and exotic foods and three-star restaurants.

The most alluring items of any cuisine are always those that are rich or fatty or starchy or sweet. I certainly would not caution a visitor to France to ignore its gastronomic wonders and glorious wines or that in merrye England one should abstain from shepherd's pie, Yorkshire pudding, and strawberry fools. But I do suggest that traveling abroad is an ideal time to fast at least one day a week. (In foreign countries it is a good idea to drink bottled water. This alone puts you into a "fasting situation.") The days you fast give you that much more time—and energy—and money!—to devote to other activities, such as shopping, sight-seeing, and walking around (always good to do while fasting).

One of my correspondents, the peripatetic Lorraine Orr, believes that fasting for a few days *before* trips abroad is an inspired notion for those who can't help traveling on their "stomach." That way, you can approach Europe's groaning boards (if you must!) lean and in good appetite.

Mrs. Orr also suggests fasting might be ideal for coping with jet lag by shortening the time required for our inner clock to synchronize with the time pattern in which we have arrived. (My co-author Jerome Agel fasts in the 24-hour period that includes a trans-Atlantic hop.)

Abroad or home, any time of the year is a good time to fast, but it's preferable where or when temperatures are warm. When no fuel is consumed, the body's thermostat is turned down a few degrees. This is why you are apt to feel chilly when you fast in the winter, even though you are indoors and in a properly heated place. The temperature outdoors will seem colder than it is; to compensate, you should dress warmly.

One excellent way to keep cool in summer is to fast. Calories generate heat.

19.

Some Often-Asked Questions

In my consultations, lectures, and media interviews around the country, certain questions about fasting recur.

I have prepared a compendium of some of these queries and my answers to them; the answers here incorporate data drawn from current research. (The two questions I'm most frequently asked—How much weight will I lose? and Will I gain back the weight after the fast?—are treated in chapter 5.)

Q.–*What is the difference between "fasting" and "starving"?*

A.–Fasting and starving are entirely different entities. But it is a distinction that eludes many people even in the medical profession; the words can not be used interchangeably. Fasting is a self-rewarding act. Starving is a disaster inflicted upon the hungry by fate or occasionally self-inflicted by the mentally disturbed. During the fast the body is well-nourished from its stored-up "preserves." Starvation begins when the body is deprived of food after the return of appetite. The average overweight person must fast about four weeks before there is return of appetite, which is the signal to break the fast and start eating again. In starvation the body craves food and, being deprived, must consume itself.

Q.–*How does the fasting process keep you from being hungry?*

A.–The body has an automatic device for suppressing

appetite. It is a compound called ketones, the broken-down products of fatty acids. When you fast, the body increases its production of ketones, which are released into the bloodstream. As the amount of ketones increases, appetite is suppressed. The return of appetite is an indication that the fast must be broken. The tongue, which is part of the elimination system, becomes coated and bad breath develops during a longer fast. These symptoms are transitory. They are indications that you are reaping the benefits of the fasting process.

Q.–*Why aren't coffee, tea, and "no-cal" beverages all right during the fast?*

A.–Coffee and tea contain caffeine and tannic acid, respectively. These stimulants excite the central nervous system at a time when the body should be at rest. They add impurities and defeat the cleansing process of the fast. Non-caloric soft drinks "pollute" the body with undesirable chemicals. Their sweet taste—though created artificially, and not by sugar—can arouse stirrings of appetite. The only permissible beverage is water —at least two quarts every day.

Q.–*Are enemas necessary?*

A.–Certainly not on a brief fast. Because they complement and facilitate the fasting process, enemas can be taken every day on the longer fast. *Before* starting a longer fast, it is desirable to take a dose of citrate of magnesia or some other purgative.

Q.–*Don't you overeat after a fast to compensate for "lost meals"?*

A.–One of the prevailing myths is that hunger is cumulative and the satisfaction of hunger only deferred. If you skip 3 meals or 6 meals or 21 meals on a one-day or two-day or a week-long fast—the thinking goes—you will gorge yourself until you've made them up. The truth is, you do *not* accumulate hunger or appetite. One way to guard against overeating after breaking the fast—and this applies to nonfasters as well—is to eat slowly and chew carefully. When you make fasting a way of life, you won't have the urge to overeat.

Q.–*What's happening in fasting research at medical centers?*

A.–A great deal. Important studies have been undertaken in Baltimore, Paris, Cleveland, Moscow, Prague, Stockholm, Houston, Dallas, Los Angeles, São Paulo, Oslo, Brussels, Toronto, Leningrad, Pittsburgh, Philadelphia, Basel, Cork, Turin, Vienna, Dundee, Ghent, Glasgow, Innsbruck, and Palo Alto. Ninety-six doctors and scientists met in Moscow for a week in 1975 to pool their knowledge on "the fasting cure of neurotic and psychiatric patients, patients with skin diseases, and some somatic diseases accompanied by neurotic and mental disturbance." New data were offered to prove the efficiency of the fasting treatment "for treating skin diseases; neurodermatitis; some forms of psoriasis, eczema, gastroenteric diseases, and polyarthritis, provided the fast and re-feeding programs are scrupulously followed." Subjects ranging in age from youngsters to octogenarians, obese and slender, sick and healthy, have been fasted in hospital conditions, in tests lasting from 24 to 33 days, to confirm and extend knowledge of the body's metabolic reactions during fasting. Levels of calcium and potassium rise promptly to normal levels when re-feeding begins. The increasing volume of research on an international "scale" is a hopeful sign the medical profession is recognizing and exploring the use of fasting in the treatment of many human dysfunctions.

Q.–*Can fasting help a chronic underweight problem?*

A.–Paradoxically, the answer is yes, though the question would be better stated, Can you lose weight to gain weight? The point is that food and nutrition are not the same thing. The amount of food taken in is not the key to the state of nutrition; the key is how much food is digested and assimilated. There's considerable evidence fasting helps the chronically underweight person to repair his assimilation functions. Though he may have failed at all previous attempts to gain weight through programs of stepped-up caloric consumption, he will find—when he breaks the fast and starts to eat again—that his food is digested more easily and absorbed more efficiently. He will be eating less than he did before the fast, but finally putting on weight.

Q.–*Can fasting blunt the effects of pollution on the city dweller?*

A.–Urban pollution is now one of the permanent facts of life. We used to think of it as confined principally to cities such as New York and Los Angeles and Pittsburgh and Tokyo. But in my recent travels, I have been appalled to see how the clouds of smog have become nearly ubiquitous, casting their poisonous shadows over such once-"pure" and lovely cities as Phoenix, Mexico City, Denver, and even Palm Springs. The urbanites may not be able to do much about the air they breathe, but a periodic fast cleanses away some of the toxins being absorbed. One of my colleagues believes fasts are *essential* for city dwellers constantly exposed to the exhausts of automobiles, chemicals belched from factory stacks, smoke from incinerators, and—in New York particularly—the gases from tons of dog dung decomposing on the sidewalks and streets.

Q.–*Does fasting turn off the taste for "the good things in life"?*

A.–The "good things in life" relating to food and eating usually mean something sweet, starchy, or alcoholic. Who among us doesn't relish an occasional cocktail or a glass of wine or an indecently rich dessert? These tastes are *not* jeopardized by fasting. As a matter of fact, the brief but regular fast is being used by some people as the way to indulge these tastes without "paying" for it, that is, without gaining weight. One friend told me, "At last I've found a way to have my cakes and ales. . . ." Or, as an amiable Georgian put it, "I don't have to change any of my bad habits. I just put them on ice one day every week." This Southern gentleman likes his bourbon highballs before dinner and such treats at the table as "finger-lickin' good" fried chicken, steaks, candied yams, and pecan pies. I certainly do not recommend items like these as staples in any diet. But if these "good things" are *that* dear to the taste buds, you can go on having them if you stick to a water-only diet one day a week.

Q.–*What is the "protein-sparing fast"?*

A.–Protein-sparing is a medical treatment, not a do-it-yourself regimen. The protein-sparing "fast" is not, strictly speaking, a fast at all; it is a modified or a supplemental fast. Its appeal seems to be to those who still hesitate about the real thing. The erroneous premise of the protein-sparing "fast" is that the total fast is dangerous. If you drink only water, that theory goes, half the weight loss would come out of lean tissues and the result would be a deterioration of muscles, inducing weakness and fatigue and possibly a host of undesirable side effects. While conceding that a total, or real, fast brings about dramatic weight losses, the doctors who devised the supplemental fast contend that protein tissues are "eaten into" concomitantly with fatty tissues when only water is consumed. *This is simply untrue!* The protein supplement comes either in the form of small amounts of lean meat, fish, or fowl, or in a bittersweet formula containing amino acids—components of protein—sometimes mixed with glucose. The meat, fish, or fowl servings may add up to a starvation diet of 700 calories a day; the prescribed amounts of the bittersweet, pre-digested protein formula may amount to 300 calories or more a day. There are reports that the modified fast is easily tolerated and that patients stick to it and achieve weight-loss goals. But the process can be prolonged, requiring daily supervision. My objection to protein-sparing is basic: there is no need for it. It delays and dilutes the benefits of fasting. The body does not begin to consume its lean tissue until the stored-up fat has been utilized. This does not occur before about four weeks of fasting. If overweight is the problem, a true fast will accomplish the loss of weight much more quickly and easily than a modified fast that permits at least 300 calories a day. If the objective is to give the body a complete rest, water alone is preferable to small amounts of food or premixed protein supplements. Anyone who has tried all the fad diets has learned *it is easier to eat nothing at all than to eat reduced rations*. And the personal rewards are much greater. For 5,000 years people have enjoyed fasting without the support of protein-sparing supplements. The promoters of these supplements are trying to board the fasting bandwagon with one foot. By the way, protein-sparing is anything but money-sparing. The treatment is expensive.

Q.–*Can fasting restore virility?*

A.–The claim is made repeatedly that it can, but documentation is hard to come by. Judging from an article in the nation's press, I would say the chance of a man overcoming his infertility through fasting would be promising if he's anything like our simian friends. The article was headlined "Casey's at Bat Again." At the Omaha Zoo a gorilla named Casey was put on a "crash" diet to get his weight down to 420 pounds (from 576). After shaping up, Casey sired a baby. Casey was then a ripe old 20—most gorillas are not potent beyond the ages of 15 to 17. The zoo director also noted that fat animals do not reproduce as well as thin animals. I am also asked if sex is all right during the fast. The answer is that it is more than all right any time both partners are so inclined. Many people, in fact, find both sexual desire and performance enhanced during a fast. Losing weight improves physical appearance, which in turn increases sexual desirability.

Q.–Can fasting lead to anorexia nervosa?

A.–Anorexia nervosa is a state of severe emotional disturbance, and often an early symptom of schizophrenia. In my regular practice I have treated many anorexics and in *not a single case* has there been a history of fasting. Here again it is the medical profession at fault for promulgating misinformation and instilling baseless fears. Doctors will warn patients who are perfectly well and emotionally stable that if they fast they may either be unable or unwilling to resume eating; *this is simply untrue.* Any person in average good health does not become anorexic by fasting. Anorexics have a delusion that they are overweight even when they have starved themselves to 80 or so pounds. They alternately starve and gorge themselves. I say "starve" because *they persistently eat small quantities of food* insufficient to support their caloric and nutritional needs. If they eat meat, they broil or fry it until it is almost completely carbonized; in other words, they burn it almost to ashes. Some anorexics have developed the dubious skill of putting a finger deep into their throat to disgorge the food before it has had time to digest and add weight. Some have become so expert at bringing up food they no longer have to use a finger. After gorging, they go to the bathroom or to the kitchen and drink so much water that vomiting is induced. I have never treated an anorexia nervosa who did not have some disturbance of glucose metabolism. A family history of diabetes is also a common finding. Anorexia nervosa is an illness encountered almost exclusively in adolescent girls; only occasionally does a male suffer from it. Anorexics do not fast—they starve.

Q.–Can fasting induce visions?

A.–The literature is replete with accounts of visions brought on by fasting. American Indians would placate their gods and "see" a benign fate awaiting them. The Bible tells us Jesus and Moses and Daniel fasted for forty days to bring on divine revelations. The disciples of Eastern mysticism fast in the hope of receiving "other-worldly" illuminations. Extraordinary truths and heavenly messages are said to be received during the extended fast. It is difficult to document this type of phenomenon. Fasts of a day or two or a week induce a tranquil and spiritual feeling, but I personally do not believe mystical visions or celestial revelations are a realistic goal for a fast of any length.

Q.–*Do you recommend the bypass operation, instead of fasting, for the extremely obese?*

A.–I categorically do not recommend the bypass operation, whose purpose is to reduce absorbing surfaces and keep the body from assimilating food. After the operation, patients experience wide mood swings, anxiety, depression, and irritability. Their necessary adjustments in life-style can strain relationships with family and friends. Principal drawbacks of the bypass procedure are the occurrence of major somatic complications, with concomitant discouragement and apprehension, and the fact that benefits may last only two to three years—they are not necessarily permanent. For the extremely obese, fasting in a hospital under supervision is preferable from every point of view.

Q.–*Can pets be fasted?*

A.–Judging from some of the fat cats and plump pooches I see *everywhere* I walk, I would say they most certainly could—and should. (Fasting, as a matter of fact, is routine for animals in the wild and for sick or injured animals.) Just as children become overweight by imitating the eating habits of their overweight parents, overfed pets seem to have masters or mistresses who are overfed. If overstuffed Fanny and petite Fifi can wear matching mink jackets, they surely can join each other in an occasional fast. Whatever Fifi has been eating, by the way, she's been eating better than her master or mistress. The pet food industry seems to lavish far more concern on packaging nutritious fare into those cans of dog and cat food than is expended on products put up for human consumption. The late J. I. Rodale, founder-publisher of *Prevention* magazine, told of being impressed by the contents on a box he picked up in a supermarket: "Meat and bone meal, ground corn with wheat germ, ground whole wheat with bran and wheat germ, soybean meal, fish meal (including glands and livers), dry milk solids, brewer's yeast, animal fat, cheese meal, sun-dried alfalfa meal, salt, powdered garlic, expertly blended and toasted. . . ." At the bottom of the box it read: "For dogs of discrimination." Mr. Rodale correctly noted that there are many undiscriminating millionaires who are not eating as well.

Q.–*How often should you fast for the best results?*
A.–Fasting brings many marvelous results. But after years of supervising fasts, I am convinced that an initial fast of whatever length—even as long as a month or until appetite returns—is not sufficient to achieve and sustain *all* the desirable goals. Fasting must become part of the way of life, especially for those who come to it originally to lose weight. It takes more than one fast to secure a revised perspective on the role of food and eating in the life of even the physically and emotionally healthy person. The first fast—regardless of its duration—can be profitably followed by fasting one day a week and one weekend a month. Many people regularly set aside one day every week. (Monday seems to be the most popular time for the one-day-a-week fast, probably to compensate for weekend indulgences.) Some people prefer a three-to-five-day fast once a month. Whatever your pattern of fasting, after an extended fast, it should not exceed a total of six days in a month. A long fast of two consecutive weeks or more should not be repeated for at least six months, and only then in a medical setting. No one should diet or fast himself or herself below the desirable weight for his or her age and height based on medical tables. And remember, no matter how long

or how frequently you fast, you should do so only with your doctor's consent.

Q.—*Does fasting prolong the life span?*

A.—Animal studies reported by Susan Seliger in *The National Observer* show that rats fed a low-protein diet one day and then fasted the next day lived 50 percent longer than normally fed rats. Dr. Charles Barrows of the National Institute of Aging discovered that this feeding pattern need not be started from birth. An adult animal put on this regimen will live longer, also. It is widely claimed in the literature that the biological process of aging is slowed by systematic fasting. Herbert Shelton, who directed tens of thousands of fasts, has reported on this phenomenon.

Q.—*If it's said by some to be a "cure-all," why isn't fasting more popular?*

A.—I disagree with the premise that fasting isn't popular. There are millions of "closet" fasters. I am constantly amazed—and pleased—to discover in my travels just how many people throughout the world are "into" fasting. At a dinner party I learned my host and three other guests—all professional people—fast one or two days every week to maintain the weight losses they achieved from a longer fast. Another indication of the growing acceptance of fasting is the widespread media interest. Within the last year there have been long articles on fasting in high-circulation periodicals like *The New York Times, Town and Country,* the Sunday supplement *Metro, Cosmopolitan, Penthouse-Forum, Playboy,* the *Los Angeles Times, The National Observer,* and *Newsday.* Even *Family Circle,* a supermarket magazine (with a circulation approaching 9,000,000) dependent on food processors for most of its advertising revenue, saw fit to publish a personal-experience feature extolling the virtues of fasting. "Not for Women Only," the nationally syndicated television program moderated by Barbara

Walters and Hugh Downs, did a two-part program on fasting; I was on the panel. Since late 1975 I have discussed fasting on radio and television stations throughout the country and have been interviewed by reporters for some of our most prestigious newspapers and magazines. The increasing worldwide acceptance of fasting makes *Fasting: The Ultimate Diet* an ongoing best seller. I have been informed that fasting retreats here and abroad are doing capacity business and have waiting lists. Fasting will become even *more* "popular" when the myths, fears, and half-truths finally evaporate.

20.

The Joys of Fasting

Fasting is easier than any diet.

Fasting is the quickest way to lose weight.

Fasting can yield weight losses of up to 20 pounds or more in the first week.

Fasting is adaptable to a busy life.

Fasting is used successfully in the treatment of many physical ills.

Fasting gives the body a physiological rest.

Fasting is a calming experience, often relieving tension and insomnia.

Fasting lowers cholesterol and blood-pressure levels.

Fasting frequently induces feelings of euphoria, a natural "high."

Fasting helps to eliminate or modify smoking, drug, and drinking addictions.

Fasting leads to improved dietary habits.

Fasting is a regulator, educating the body to consume only as much food as it needs.

Fasting increases the pleasure of eating.

Fasting produces "found" time—all the hours spent in marketing, preparing, and consuming food and drink.

Fasting is a rejuvenator, slowing the aging process.

Fasting is an energizer, not a debilitator.

Fasting often results in a more vigorous sex life.

Fasting aids in the elimination process.

Fasting rids the body of toxins, giving it an "internal shower."

Fasting does *not* deprive the body of essential nutrients.

Fasting can be used to uncover the sources of food allergies.

Fasting is used effectively in the treatment of schizophrenia and other mental ills.

Fasting under proper supervision can be tolerated easily for anywhere up to four weeks.

Fasting does not accumulate appetite; hunger "pangs" disappear after a day or two.

Fasting is routine for the animal kingdom.

Fasting has been a commonplace experience for man almost as long as he has been eating.

Fasting is a rite in all religions; the Bible alone has 74 references to it.

Fasting under proper conditions is absolutely safe.

Fasting is *not* starving.

Bibliography

Acers, Elva S. Letter to Jerome Agel, May 22, 1976.

Airola, Paavo O. *There Is a Cure for Arthritis.* West Nyack, N.Y.: Parker, 1968.

Allen, Hannah. *The Happy Truth About Protein,* Pearsall, Texas: Healthway Publications.

American Dietetic Association Report. "Position Paper on Food and Nutrition Misinformation on Selected Topics." *Journal of the American Dietetic Association* 66 (3) 1975: 277–80.

Aoki, Thomas T., et al. "Effect of Glucagon on Amino Acid and Nitrogen Metabolism in Fasting Man." *Metabolism: Clinical and Experimental* 23 (9) 1974: 805–14.

———. "Metabolic Effects of Glucose in Brief and Prolonged Fasted Man." *American Journal of Clinical Nutrition* 28 (5) 1975: 507–11.

Arguello, Carlos R. Letters to Jerome Agel, Jan. 30 and March 3, 1976.

Bagdade, J. D., et al. "Basal and Stimulated Hyperinsulinism: Reversible Metabolic Sequelae of Obesity." *Journal of Laboratory and Clinical Medicine* 83 (4) 1974: 563–69.

Balasse, E. O. and Neef, M. A. "Inhibition of Ketogenesis by Ketone Bodies in Fasting Humans." *Metabolism: Clinical and Experimental* 24 (9) 1975: 999–1008.

Ballantyne, F. C., et al. "Albumin Metabolism in Fasting, Obese Subjects." *British Journal of Nutrition* 30 (3) 1973: 585–92.

Barrett, Peter V. D. "Hyperbilirubinemia of Fasting." *Journal of the American Medical Association* 217 (10) 1971: 1349–53.

Benson, J. W. Jr., et al. "Glucose Utilization by Sweat Glands During Fasting in Man." *Journal of Investigative Dermatology* 63 (3) 1974: 287–91.

Berman, Steve. "Fasting: An Old Cure for Fat, A New Treatment for Schizophrenia." *Prevention,* Jan. 1976: 27–31.

Blackburn, George L. Letter to Jerome Agel, March 4, 1976.

Blackburn, George L., et al. "Protein Sparing Therapy During

Periods of Starvation with Sepsis or Trauma." *Annals of Surgery* 177 (5) 1973: 588–94.

Block, Marshall B. "Hypoglycemia: Clinical Implications. Part II: Fasting Hypoglycemia." *Arizona Medicine* 32 (1) 1975: 37–39.

Bolzano, K., et al. "Effect of Total Starvation on Cardiac Output of Overweight Women with Normal Circulation." *Wiener Klinische Wochenschrift* 85 (40) 1973: 657–61.

Boulter, Philip R. Letter to Jerome Agel, May 24, 1976.

Boulter, Philip R., et al. "Dissociation of the Renin-Aldosterone System and Refractoriness to the Sodium-Retaining Action of Mineralocorticoid During Starvation in Man." *Journal of Clinical Endocrinology and Metabolism* 38 (2) 1974: 248–54.

———. "Effect of Aldosterone Blockade During Fasting and Refeeding." *American Journal of Clinical Nutrition* 26 (April) 1973: 397–402.

———. "Pattern of Sodium Excretion Accompanying Starvation." *Metabolism: Clinical and Experimental* 22 (5) 1973: 675–82.

Bricklin, Mark. "Color His Face Red 2." *Prevention,* April 1976: 78.

Brodie, Franklin. Letter to the Editor, *The New York Times Magazine,* Dec. 15, 1974: 35.

Brody, Jane E. "Additional Evidence Indicates That Diet Is a Cancer Cause." *The New York Times,* Dec. 2, 1975: 1+.

Brosius, Dorothy K. Letter to Jerome Agel. (undated)

Burros, Marian. "Our Food: Refined Way to Die?" *The Washington Post,* Oct. 23, 1975.

———. "Pet Food: A Dietary Staple for Impoverished Americans." *The Washington Post,* Dec. 7, 1975: D2.

Busse Grawitz, P. Letter to Jerome Agel (undated).

Cady, Steve. "Olympic Diet: Hold the Steak, Vitamins." *The New York Times,* June 11, 1976: D13+.

Cahill, Kathleen. Letter to Jerome Agel from Oxfam-America, Dec. 6, 1976.

Calloway, Doris Howes. "Recommended Dietary Allowances for Protein and Energy." *Journal of the American Dietetic Association* 64 (Feb.) 1974: 157–62.

Carter, Michelle. "Try Fasting for Weight Control." *San Mateo* (Calif.) *Times,* Sept. 30, 1975.

Carter, William J., et al. "Effect of Thyroid Hormone on Metabolic Adaptation to Fasting." *Metabolism: Clinical and Experimental* 24 (10) 1975: 1175–83.

Cerra, Frances. "Parents Close Top on Sodas in Westchester School Menu." *The New York Times,* Feb. 3, 1976: 33.

Chandler, Russell. "A Life of Freedom in 'Voluntary Poverty,' " *The Washington Post,* Dec. 14, 1975: D2.

Chandler, Stephen T. Letter to Allan Cott, June 18, 1975.

Chaussain, J. L. Letter to Jerome Agel, April 7, 1976.

——. "Glycemic Response to 24-Hour Fast in Normal Children and Children with Ketotic Hypoglycemia." *Journal of Pediatrics* 82 (3) 1973: 438–43.

Chaussain, J. L., et al. "Effect of Fast in Normal Children: Influence of Age." Unpublished paper.

——. "Effect of 24-Hour Fast in Obese Children." Unpublished paper.

——. "Glycemic Response to 24-Hour Fast in Normal Children and Children with Ketotic Hypoglycemia: II. Hormonal and Metabolic Changes." *Journal of Pediatrics* 85 (6) 1974: 776–81.

Cheatham, R. J. Letter to Jerome Agel, May 14, 1976.

Cherry, Rona. "McDonald's Goes to School in Arkansas." *The New York Times*, Sept. 30, 1976.

Chesney, Peter J. "Tyringham Naturopathic Clinic." Reprinted from *Here's Health*.

Christophe, A. Letters to Jerome Agel, June 9 and Sept. 23, 1976.

Christophe, A. and Verdonk, G. "Effect of Prolonged Fasting on Serum Lipids and Serum Lipo-proteins in Obese Men." *Hoppe-Seyler's Zeitschrift für Physiologische Chemii* 355 (10) 1974: 1184.

Cincinnati Enquirer, The. "Well-Padded Women Belie Diet, Spa Fads." June 1, 1976: 1.

Clancy, Mary Louise. "Fasting Gains New-Found Popularity." *Twin Circle*, Dec. 14, 1975.

Clark, Michael. "Franconia, Maybe What a College Ought to Be. *Prevention*, August 1976.

Clements, F. W. "Nutrition 11: Recommended Dietary Allowances." *Medical Journal of Australia* 62–2 (1) 1975: 24–26.

Cockburn, Alexander and Ridgeway, James. "The Greasy Pole." *The Village Voice*, May 31, 1976.

Committee on Nutritional Misinformation. "Vegetarian Diets." National Academy of Sciences, May 1974.

Conners, Bernard F. *Don't Embarrass the Bureau.* New York: Avon, 1973.

Cooper, Donald L., with Fair, Jeff. "Pregame Meal: To Eat or Not to Eat—and What?" *The Physician and Sportsmedicine*, Nov. 1975.

Costill, David L. Letter to Jerome Agel, Nov. 2, 1976.

Cott, Allan with Agel, Jerome and Boe, Eugene. *Fasting: The Ultimate Diet.* New York: Bantam, 1975.

Cott, Allan. "Controlled Fasting Treatment for Schizophrenia." *The Journal of Orthomolecular Psychiatry* 3 (4) 1974: 301–11.

Cravetto, C. A., et al. "Metabolic Aspects of Prolonged Fasting in Obese Subjects." *Folia Endocrinologica* 26 (2) 1973: 139–52.

Crosby, William H. "Can a Vegetarian Be Well Nourished?"
    Journal of the American Medical Association 233 (8) 1975:
    898.

Damon, G. Edward. "A Primer on Dietary Minerals." *FDA
    Consumer*, Sept. 1974.

————. "A Primer on Food Additives." *FDA Consumer*,
    May 1973.

————. "A Primer on Four Nutrients: Proteins, Carbo-
    hydrates Fats, and Fiber." *FDA Consumer*, Feb. 1975.

Davis, Gwen. Letter to Jerome Agel, March 22, 1976.

de Saumarez, Lady Julia. Letters to Jerome Agel, March 17
    and April 13, 1976.

Dept. of Health, Education and Welfare. Letter to Jerome
    Agel, Sept. 3, 1976.

Dosti, Rose. "Fasting? See Your Doctor." *Los Angeles Times*,
    Nov. 13, 1975: IV,1.

Dougherty, Paul, "High-Speed Juice Diet Helps Star Man Lose
    12 Lbs. in Just Six Days." *The Star*, June 8, 1976: 9.

Downs, Hugh. Letter to Jerome Agel, March 1, 1976.

Drenick, E. J., et al. "Energy Expenditure in Fasting Obese
    Men." *Journal of Laboratory and Clinical Medicine* 81 (3)
    1973: 421–30.

Duran, Mary. "Fasting Improves Health." *Atlantic City* (N.J.)
    Press, Sept. 7, 1975.

Dusky, Lorraine. "Fasting on the Run." *Town and Country*,
    July 1975.

Dwyer, Johanna. "Protein: Why You Need It. Where You Get
    It." *Redbook* 144 (March) 1975: 85+.

Dwyer, Johanna, et al. "The New Vegetarians: The Natural
    High?" *Journal of the American Dietetic Association* 65
    (Nov.) 1974: 529–36.

Erhard, Darla. "Nutrition Education for the 'Now' Genera-
    tion." *Journal of Nutrition Education* 2 (4) 1971: 135–39.

Ettenberg, Selma. Letter to Jerome Agel (undated).

Ewald, Ellen Buchman. *Recipes for a Small Planet*. New
    York: Ballantine, 1973.

Fineberg, Seymour K. "The Realities of Obesity and Fad
    Diets." *Nutrition Today*, July/Aug. 1972: 23.

Fleming, Laura W. and Stewart, W. K. "Effect of Carbo-
    hydrate Intake on the Urinary Excretion of Magnesium,
    Calcium, and Sodium in Fasting Obese Patients," *Nephron*
    16 (1) 1976: 64–73.

Fogel, Suzanne. Letter to Jerome Agel, June 1, 1976.

Food for Fitness. Mt. View, Calif.: World Publications, 1975.

Forbes, Gilbert B. "Weight Loss During Fasting: Implications
    for the Obese." *The American Journal of Clinical Nutri-
    tion* 23 (9) 1970: 1212–19.

Ford, Norman. "I Travel for Health." *Prevention*, June 1976:
    94–101.

————. Letters to Jerome Agel, May 15 and June 6, 1976.

Fremon, David. "Fasting for Fun and Peril." *Chicago Sun-Times Midwest Magazine*, June 8, 1975: 15–16.

Freour, P., et al. "Blood Alcohol and the Consumption of Alcoholic Beverages Fasting and During a Meal." *Revue d'Epidémiologie Médecine Sociale et Santé Publique* 20 (8) 1972: 757–71.

Friggens, Paul. "The Corn That Could Change the Lives of Millions." *Reader's Digest* 106 (633) 1975: 144–48.

Fry, T. C. *Program for Dynamic Health.* Chicago: Natural Hygiene Press, 1974.

————. *Superior Foods, Diet Principles and Practices for Perfect Health.* Pearsall, Texas: Healthway Publications.

Gedde-Dahl, D. "Fasting Serum Gastrin Levels in Humans with Low Pentagastrin-Stimulated Gastric Acid Secretion." *Scandinavian Journal of Gastroenterology* 9 (6) 1974: 597–99.

Gelman, A., et al. "Role of Metabolic Acidosis on Renal Function During Starvation." *American Journal of the Medical Sciences* 266 (1) 1973: 33–36.

Genuth, Saul M., et al. "Weight Reduction in Obesity by Outpatient Semistarvation." *Journal of the American Medical Association* 230 (7) 1974: 987–91.

Gilbert, C. H. and Galton, D. J. "The Effect of Catecholamines and Fasting on Cyclic-AMP and Release of Glycerol from Human Adipose Tissues." *Hormone and Metabolic Research* 6 (3) 1974: 229–33.

Glasser, Ronald J. "Being a Medical Hero Can Be Hell" (excerpt from *The Body Is the Hero*). *Prevention*, May 1976: 70–76.

Goeschke, H. and Lauffenburger, T. "Breath Acetone and Ketone in Normal and Overweight Subjects During Total Fasting." *Research in Experimental Medicine* 165 (3) 1975: 233–44.

Goeschke, H., et al. "Nitrogen Loss in Normal and Obese Subjects During Total Fast." *Klinische Wochenschrift* 53 (13) 1975: 605–10.

Good Housekeeping Institute. "Foods That Give the Most Protein for Your Money." *Good Housekeeping* 179 (Nov.) 1974: 244+.

Gordon, John Steele. Letter to the Editor, *The New York Times Magazine*, Dec. 15, 1974: 35.

Gravenhorst, A. G. Letter to Jerome Agel, Feb. 24, 1976.

Graydon, J. Graeme. Letter to Jerome Agel, May 25, 1976.

Greenblatt, David J., et al. "Bioavailability of Digoxin Tablets and Elixir in the Fasting and Postprandial States." *Clinical Pharmacology and Therapeutics* 16 (3, Part I) 1974: 444–48.

Grotta-Kurska, Daniel. "Before You Say 'Baloney' . . . Here's What You Should Know About Vegetarianism." *Today's Health* 52 (10) 1974: 18+.

————. "Do We Eat Too Much Meat?" *Reader's Digest* 106 (634) 1975: 195–200.

Gussow, Joan. Conversation with Eugene Boe, June 1, 1976.

Halperin, Mitchell L., et al. "Effects of Fasting on the Control of Fatty-Acid Synthesis in Hepatoma 777 and Host Liver: Role of Long-Chain Fatty Acyl-COA, the Metochondrial Citrate Transporter and Pyruvate Behydrogenase Activity." *European Journal of Biochemistry* 50 (3) 1975: 517–22.

Hammer, Leon I. Letter to Jerome Agel, May 20, 1976.

Hansen, A. and Weeke, J. "Fasting Serum Growth Hormone Levels and Growth Hormone Responses in Exercise During Normal Menstrual Cycles and Cycles of Oral Contraceptives." *Scandinavian Journal of Clinical and Laboratory Investigation* 34 (3) 1974: 199–205.

Hardinge, Mervyn G. "Raising Infant on Vegetarian Diet." Questions and Answers, *Journal of the American Medical Association* 227 (1) 1974: 88.

Hardinge, Mervyn G. and Crooks, Hulda. "Non-Flesh Dietaries." *Journal of the American Dietetic Association* 43 (6) 1963: 545–58.

Hardinge, Mervyn G. and Stare, Frederick J. "Nutritional Studies of Vegetarians." *The Journal of Clinical Nutrition* 2 (2) 1954: 73–88.

Harper's Weekly. "Mac the Knife." May 31, 1976.

"Health Hydros and Farms in England." English Tourist Board, Information 12.

Hedner, Pavo, et al. "Insulin Release in Fasting Man Induced by Impure but Not by Pure Preparations of Cholecystokinin." *ACTA Medica Scandinavica* 97 (1–2) 1975: 109–112.

Heesen, H., et al. "Thiamin and Thiamin Pyrophosphate in Obese Patients on Reducing Diet and Complete Fasting." *Deutsche Medizinische Wochenschrift* 100 (11) 1975: 544–48.

Heyden, S., et al. "Weight Reduction in Adolescents." *Nutrition and Metabolism* 15 (4/5) 1973: 295–304.

Hill, John W. Letter to Jerome Agel, May 7, 1976.

Hoffer, A. Review of *Fasting: The Ultimate Diet*, 1976.

Hurst, Lynda. "How You Can Lose Weight Fast." *Toronto Star*, Oct. 30, 1976: F-1.

Illich, Ivan. *Medical Nemesis*. New York: Pantheon, 1976.

James, George. " '75 High Jumper Falls Free." *New York News*, July 23, 1976: 5.

Jones, J. J. and Gelfand, M. "Fasting Serum Lipoproteins in Rural Africans in Rhodesia, Measured by Filtration and Nephelometry." *Clinica Chimica ACTA* 57 (2) 1974: 131–34.

Journal of the American Dietetic Association. "Obesity and Unemployment." 65 (Feb.) 1974: 162.

————. "Vegetarian Diets." 65 (Aug.) 1974: 121–22.

Journal of the American Medical Association. "Obesity: A Continuing Enigma." 211 (3) 1970: 493.

Kalkhoff, R. K. and Kim, H. J. "Metabolic Responses to Fasting and Ethanol Infusion in Obese Diabetic Subjects. Relationship to Insulin Deficiency." *Diabetes* 22 (5) 1973: 372–80.

Kinderlehrer, Jane. "Students Do Better with A-Plus Food." *Prevention,* June 1976: 70–73.

Kirban, Salem. *How to Keep Healthy and Happy by Fasting.* Huntingdon Valley, Penna.: Salem Kirban Inc., 1976.

Kolanowski, J., et al. "Further Evaluation of the Role of Insulin in Sodium Retention Associated with Carbohydrate Administration after a Fast in the Obese." *European Journal of Clinical Investigation* (2) 1972: 439–44.

————. "Hormonal Adaptation to Short-Term Total Fast in the Obese." *Médecin et Hygiène* 1975: 112–16.

————. "Influence of Fasting on Adrenocortical and Pancreatic Islet Response to Glucose Loads in the Obese." *European Journal of Clinical Investigation* (1) 1970: 25–31.

————. "Influence of Glucagon on Sodium (Na) Balance During Fasting and Carbohydrate Refeeding in the Obese." *European Journal of Clinical Investigation* in *European Society for Clinical Investigation Abstracts* 3 (3) 1973: 244–45.

————. "Metabolic and Hormonal Effects of Short-Term Total Starvation in Obesity." *Schweizerische Medizinische Wochenschrift* 104 (29) 1974: 1022–28.

————. "Sodium Balance and Renal Tubular Sensitivity to Aldosterone During Total Fast and Carbohydrate Refeeding in the Obese." *European Journal of Clinical Investigation* (6) 1976: 75–83.

Kolata, G. B. "Brain Biochemistry: Effects of Diet." *Science* 192 (Apr. 2) 1976: 41–42.

Kuhn, E. "Renal Response to a Water Load in Normal Fasting Subjects." *Nutrition and Metabolism* 16 (3) 1974: 163–71.

Ladies Home Journal. "The Main Course Takes New Course: Lots to Eat Without the Meat." 91 (March) 1974: 86+.

Lanza, Karen. Letter to Jerome Agel, May 19, 1976.

Lappé, Frances Moore. *Diet for a Small Planet.* New York: Ballantine, 1971.

Leigh, Robin. "Fasting: The Ultimate Diet," a review, *Sun Reporter,* Sept. 20, 1975.

Leighty, John M. "The Many Benefits of Fasting." *Newhall* (Calif.) *Signal,* Nov. 12, 1975.

Levick, Diane. "Junk Food Junkies Could Kick Habit at Beach." *Fairpress* (Westport, Conn.), July 14, 1976: 4a.

Lewis, George. Letter to Allan Cott, Aug. 6, 1975.

————. Letter to Jerome Agel, March 10, 1976.

Lewis, Harold. "The Sure Way to Lose Weight—When All Else Fails." *National Enquirer,* Oct. 26, 1975.

Lilly, John C. Letter to Jerome Agel, June 1, 1976.

Liporetskii, B. M. and Ryzhov, V. M. "Changes in Free Fatty Acid Levels and Triglyceride in Blood After Fasting and Food Loads in the Assessing Lipid Metabolism in Patients with Atherosclerosis." *Kardiologiya* 14 (5) 1974: 40–43.

Love, Sam. "A Delicious Collection of Essays for the 'Real Food' Movement." *The Washington Post,* Oct. 16, 1976: B-2.

MacFadyen, U. M., et al. "Starvation and Human Slow-Wave Sleep." *Journal of Applied Physiology* 35 (3) 1973: 391–94.

McKinney, Joan. "It's a Fast Way to Lose That Weight." *Oakland* (Calif.) *Tribune,* Aug. 29, 1975: 30.

Majumder, Sanat K. "Vegetarianism: Fad, Faith or Fact." *American Scientist* 60, 1972: 175–179.

Mann, George V. "Raising Infant on Vegetarian Diet," Questions and Answers, *Journal of the American Medical Association* 227 (1) 1974: 88.

Marks, Marjorie. "This Door Leads to Better Food for Teens." *Prevention,* Dec. 1976: 142.

Mayer, Jean. "The Practical Way to Learn." *The Washington Post,* Oct. 23, 1975: D6.

Mayer, Jean and Dwyer, Johanna. "Vegetarianism—Healthy Way of Life." *New York News,* Dec. 8, 1976: 58.

Maynard, Joyce. "Abstinence Without Tears." *The New York Times,* Nov. 10, 1976.

Mehta, Ved. "Mahatma Gandhi and His Apostles," Part II. *The New Yorker,* May 17, 1976.

Mercer, Marilyn. "More Protein for Your Money." *McCall's,* Feb. 1975: 43.

Merimee, T. J. and Tyson, John E. "Stabilization of Plasma Glucose During Fasting." *New England Journal of Medicine* 291 (24) 1974: 1275–78.

Miller, D. S. and Payne, P. R. "Weight Maintenance and Food Intake." *Journal of Nutrition* 78, 1962: 255–62.

Miller, Don Ethan. "How I Tried to Fast for a Week and Lived." *The Village Voice,* May 3, 1976: 27.

Miller, James C. Letter to Jerome Agel.

Minneapolis Tribune. "Looking Back on Being Raised as a Lady." May 30, 1976.

Moore, John G. Letter to Jerome Agel, May 10, 1976.

Moore, William. "Brown's Strange Eating Habits." *San Francisco Chronicle,* March 5, 1976: 1+.

————. Letter to Jerome Agel, June 11, 1976.

Myerson, Bess. "How to Beat Junk Food 'Machine.'" *New York News,* Aug. 4, 1976.

National Catholic Welfare Conference. *Poenitemini: Apostolic Constitution on Fast and Abstinence.* Feb. 17, 1966.

National Dairy Council. "Health Implications of Fad Reducing Diets." *Dairy Council Digest* 37 (2) 1966: 7–10.

"NBC Reports: What Is This Thing Called Food?" Sept. 8, 1976.

Nelson, Ralph A. "What Should Athletes Eat? Unmixing Folly and Facts." *The Physician and Sportsmedicine,* Nov. 1975: 67–72.

New Times. "The Diet that Drives You to Drink." April 1, 1976: 20.

New York News. "Caroline Hit by Disorder of the Stomach." April 30, 1976.

———. "Casey's at Bat Again." Feb. 11, 1976.

———. "Gilmore Will Get His 3rd Date With Death." Dec. 15, 1976.

New York Times, The. "Is Travel Really Broadening?" Feb. 15, 1976: VII, 1.

———. "New Scale Can Detect Bite-Sized Weight Gain." June 4, 1976.

New Yorker, The. "Talk of the Town: Fast." Jan. 19, 1976: 21–22.

———. May 17, 1976. p. 120.

News (Mexico City). "Doctor Welch." March 5, 1976: 18.

Nicolayev, Yuri. Letters to Jerome Agel, April 22 and May 6, 1976.

———. Summary of Conference at Moscow Psychiatric Institute on Fasting Cure, May 13–15, 1975.

Nicolayev, Yuri and Rudakov, Y. Y. "Psychobiological Training of Human Regulatory Protective and Adaptive Mechanisms." *Biologie Aviakosm Medicine* 9 (1) 1975: 86–88.

Nilsson, L. H. and Hultman, E. "Liver Glycogen in Man—the Effect of Total Starvation or a Carbohydrate-Poor Diet Followed by Carbohydrate Refeeding." *Scandinavian Journal of Clinical and Laboratory Investigation* 32 (4) 1973: 325–30.

North, K. A. K., et al. "The Mechanisms by Which Sodium Excretion Is Increased During a Fast but Reduced on Subsequent Carbohydrate Feeding." *Clinical Science and Molecular Medicine* 46 (4) 1974: 423–32.

Not For Women Only. "Fasting/Dieting/Eating," television syndicated series.

Novich, Max M. Letter to Jerome Agel, April 20, 1976.

Null, Gary. "Fasting." *Let's Live,* Nov. 1975: 84–89.

Null, Gary and Staff. *The Complete Question and Answer Book of General Nutrition.* New York: Dell, 1974.

Nutrition Reviews. "FAO/WHO Handbook on Human Nutritional Requirements, 1974." 33 (5) 1975: 147–51.

———. "Fasting for Obese Children." 26 (11) 1968: 335–36.

———. "Food Faddism." 32 (Supplement) 1974: 53.

O'Connell, R. C. "Nitrogen Conservation in Starvation: Graded Responses to Intravenous Glucose." *Journal of Clinical Endocrinology and Metabolism* 39 (3) 1974: 555–63.

Oles, Michael. Letter to the Editor, *The Village Voice*, May 17, 1976: 6.

Orr, Lorraine. Letter to Jerome Agel, 1976.

Oxfamnews. "Fast for a World Harvest Gives U.S. a Taste of Hunger." 1 (1) 1975: 1+.

———. "Oxfam's Nov. 20 Fast Focuses National Spotlight on Hunger." 2 (1) 1976.

Parrish, John B. "Implications of Changing Food Habits for Nutrition Educators." *Journal of Nutrition Education* 2 (4) 1971: 140–46.

Perry, Jean. "Bottled Water Floods Market." *New York News,* Oct. 19, 1976: 39.

Physical Culture. 85 (5) 1941: 57.

———. 85 (6) 1941: 4–5.

Pines, Maya. "Meatless, Guiltless." *The New York Times Magazine,* Nov. 24, 1974: 48+.

Pinsof, Barbara. Letter to Jerome Agel, April 11, 1976.

Porter, Sylvia. "Monitoring School Meals." *New York Post,* April 29, 1976: 30.

Prevention. "A Holistic Coach." June 1976: 93.

———. "Junk Food Is More than a Bad Joke." Oct. 1976: 80.

———. "J. I. Rodale Said It." May 1976: 77.

———. "Let's Give Our Children a Taste of Honest Food (For a Change!)." May 1976: 127+.

———. "Upgrading School Lunches—One Town's Response." Oct. 1976: 12.

———. "West Virginia Expels Junk Food From Public Schools." April 1976: 91.

———. Feb 1976: 92 and 179.

———. April 1976: 146.

Randal, Judith. "Fat-Stuffed Diets Are Panned as Factor in Cancer." *New York News,* Dec. 12, 1976: 16.

Raper, Nancy R. and Hill, Mary M. "Vegetarian Diets." *Nutrition Program News,* U.S. Department of Agriculture, July/Aug. 1973.

Raskin, Philip, et al. "Effect of Insulin Glucose Infusions on Plasma Glucagon Levels in Fasting Diabetics and Non-Diabetics." *Journal of Clinical Investigation* 56 (5) 1975: 1132–38.

Rath, R. and Masek, J. "Changes in the Nitrogen Metabolism in Obese Women after Fasting and Refeeding." *Metabolism: Clinical and Experimental* 15 (1) 1966: 1–8.

Rath, R., et al. "Catecholamines and Obesity, Fasting and the Adrenergic System." *Endokrinologie* 62 (2) 1973: 225–33.

————. "Relationship of Lipid and Carbohydrate Metabolism in Women During Fasting." *Review of Czechoslovak Medicine* 13 (4) 1967: 231–37.

Register, U. D. and Sonnenberg, L. M. "The Vegetarian Diet." *Journal of the American Dietetic Association* 62 (3) 1973: 253–61.

Rensberger, Boyce. "Nutrition Panel Urges Studies to Spur Production of Protein." *The New York Times*, Dec. 20, 1975: 30.

Romney, George. Letter to Jerome Agel, June 12, 1976.

Rosenbaum, Ken. "Overeaters, Here's Fast, Fast Relief." *Cleveland Press*, Sept. 26, 1975: 27.

Ross, Shirley. *Fasting*. New York: St. Martin's, 1975.

Runcie, J. and Hilditch, T. E. "Energy Provision, Tissue Utilization, and Weight Loss in Prolonged Starvation." *British Medical Journal* 2 (5915) 1974: 352–56.

Runner's World Magazine. "The Runner's Diet." Booklet of the Month, No. 14, 1972.

Sakr, Ahmad. "Fasting in Islam." *Journal of the American Dietetic Association* 67 (1) 1975: 17–21.

San Francisco Examiner. Feb. 27, 1976: 19.

Sanders, Mary Jane. "Voluntary Fasting Cures Many Ills." *Post-Tribune* (Gary, Ind.), Sept. 5, 1975.

Sapir, D. G. and Owen, O. E. "Renal Conservation of Ketone Bodies During Starvation." *Metabolism: Clinical and Experimental* 24 (1) 1975: 23–33.

Sapir, D. G., et al. "Nitrogen Sparing Induced by a Mixture of Essential Amino Acids Given Chiefly as Their Keto-Analogues During Prolonged Starvation in Obese Subjects." *Journal of Clinical Investigation* 54 (4) 1974: 974–80.

Sassoon, Beverly and Vidal. *A Year of Beauty and Health*. New York: Simon and Schuster, 1975.

Saudek, C. D., et al. "The Natriuretic Effect of Glucagon and Its Role in Starvation." *Journal of Clinical Endocrinology and Metabolism* 36 (4) 1973: 761–65.

Sauer, Georgia. "Lose Weight, Not Shirt: A Guide to Nearby Reducing Spas." *New York Sunday News*, May 16, 1976: 31+.

Schlick, W., et al. "Energy Exchange During Total Starvation." *Medizin und Ernährung* 13 (10) 1972: 215–20.

Seiberling, Dorothy. "The Art-Martyr." *New York*, May 24, 1976.

Selinger, Susan. "Fasting: An Idea to Chew On." *The National Observer*, Dec. 11, 1976: 1.

Seventeen. "Breakfast of Champions?" April 1976: 170+.

Shelton, Herbert M. *Fasting Can Save Your Life*. Chicago: Natural Hygiene Press, 1964.

————. *Fasting for Renewal of Life*. Chicago: Natural Hygiene Press, 1974.

————. *Food Combining . . . Made Easy* (Dr. Shelton's Health School).

Sidhwa, Keki R. Letters to Jerome Agel, March 20 and April 5, 1976.

Sigler, M. H. "The Mechanism of the Natriuresis of Fasting." *Journal of Clinical Investigation* 55 (2) 1975: 377–87.

Silverstein, Philip. Letter to Allan Cott, Aug. 20, 1975.

————. Letter to Jerome Agel. (undated)

Slany, J., et al. "Cardiovascular Effects of Starvation in Obese Subjects." *Wiener Klinische Wochenschrift* 86 (15) 1974: 423–28.

Spahn, U. and Plenert, W. "Changes in the Body Composition of Obese Children During Absolute Starvation." *Zeitschrift für Kinderheilkunde* 115 (1) 1973: 59–69.

Spahn, U., et al. "Changes in Parameters Appertaining to Lipolysis in Obese Children during a Weight-Reducing Regimen." *Zeitschrift für Kinderheilkunde* 114, 1973: 131–42.

Spark, Richard F. Letter to Jerome Agel, April 28, 1976.

Spark, Richard F., et al. "Renin, Aldosterone and Glucagon in the Natriuresis of Fasting." *New England Journal of Medicine* 292 (June 19) 1975: 1335–40.

Spitze, Hazel Taylor. "Innovative Techniques for Teaching Nutrition." *Journal of Nutrition Education* 2 (4) 1971: 156–58.

Steinman, Marion. "Beauty: From the Inside Out." *The New York Times Magazine*, Feb. 29, 1976: 60+.

Stephenson, Marilyn. "Making Food Labels More Informative." *FDA Consumer*, Sept. 1974.

Stern, Judith S. "How to Stay Well on a Vegetarian Diet and Save Money Too!" *Vogue* 165 (Feb.) 1975: 151.

Stewart, W. K. and Fleming, L. W. "Relationship Between Plasma and Erythrocyte Magnesium and Potassium Concentrations in Fasting Obese Subjects." *Metabolism: Clinical and Experimental* 22 (4) 1973: 535–47.

Stinebaugh, Bobby J. "Taste Thresholds for Salt in Fasting Patients." *American Journal of Clinical Nutrition* 28 (8) 1975: 814–17.

Stone, Sebastian. Letter to Jerome Agel, 1976.

Stry, David. Letter to Jerome Agel, March 5, 1976.

Stuckey, William K. "The 'No-Aging Diet': Something Fishy Here." *New York*, Oct. 11, 1976: 73.

Stunkard, Albert J. and Rush, John. "Dieting and Depression Re-examined: A Critical Review of Untoward Responses During Weight Reduction for Obesity." *Annals of Internal Medicine* 81 (4) 1974: 526–33.

Taylor, Henry Longstreet, et al. "The Effects of Successive Fasts on the Ability of Men to Withstand Fasting During Hard Work." *American Journal of Physiology* 143 (1) 1945: 148–55.

Thornton, Kellen C. "Steak, Too, Can Be 'Junk Food,'" *Fergus Falls* (Minn.) *Journal*, July 28, 1976.

Thornton, William M. Letter to Allan Cott, Aug. 23, 1975.

————. Letter to Jerome Agel, April 20, 1976.

Time. "Dieting by Starving." Nov. 22, 1976: 53.

————. "The Joy of Aging." Nov. 8, 1976: 86.

Tom, Gail and Rucker, Margaret. "Fat, Full, and Happy: Effects of Food Deprivation, External Cues, and Obesity on Preference Ratings, Consumption, and Buying Intentions." *Journal of Personality and Social Psychology* 32 (5) 1975: 761–66.

Trask, Debra. Letter and Data to Eugene Boe, Oct. 1, 1976.

Trecker, Barbara. "Fasting: A Dangerous Diet?" *New York Post*, April 26, 1975.

Trenchard, P. M. and Jennings, R. D. "Diurnal Variation in Glucose Tolerance and Its Reversal by Lengthened Fasting." *British Medical Journal* 2 (5920) 1974: 640–42.

Ubell, Earl. "Hyperkinesis: Pep Pills to Quiet the Over-Peppy Child." *The New York Times*, March 14, 1971.

Unger, Andrew. "Fasting: A Fast Way to Lose—If You Can Stomach It." *Moneysworth*, Jan. 1976.

United States Catholic Conference. *Our Daily Bread, Vol. II.* Sept. 1975.

United States Department of Health, Education and Welfare. *Obesity and Health*, Chapter 7: "Treatment Guidelines for Successful Treatment."

United States Departments of Agriculture and Health, Education and Welfare. "Food Is More Than Just Something to Eat."

Van Lear, Denise. "Come Fast With Me," a fasting account submitted to Jerome Agel, May 8, 1976.

Vidalon, C., et al. "Age-related Changes in Growth Hormone in Non-diabetic Women." *Journal of the American Geriatrics Society* 21 (6) 1973: 253–55.

Village Voice. "Food in Thought." May 31, 1976: 19.

Villas, Tennyson. Letter to Jerome Agel, March 1, 1976.

W. "The Delights of Fasting." Nov. 14–21, 1975: 24–25.

Walsh, C. H., et al. "Effect of Different Periods of Fasting on Oral Glucose Tolerance." *British Medical Journal* 2 (5868) 1973: 691–93.

Walter, R. D., et al. "The Effect of Adrenergic Blockade on the Glucagon Responses to Starvation and Hypoglycemia in Man." *Journal of Clinical Investigation* 54 (5) 1974: 1214–20.

Ward, Jack T. Letter to Jerome Agel, March 1, 1976.

Washington Post, The. "The Price of Meat." June 21, 1975: A 12.

Waters, Enoc P. "Plentiful Protein from the Sea." *FDA Consumer*, Nov. 1973.

Weber, Melva. "Weight-Loss Fast." *Vogue,* Jan. 1976: 107+.

Weinberg, Alfred F. Letter to Jerome Agel (undated).

Wesselhoeft, Conrad. "The Lewis and Clark Expedition Into Natural Foods." *Prevention,* April 1976: 126–31.

Wetzel, Betty. Letters to Jerome Agel from Oxfam-America, April 27 and May 1, 1976.

White, Philip L. "At Last, the Ultimate Diet: Total Fasting (Total Foolishness)." *American Medical News,* Jan. 19, 1976: 4.

Wigmore, Ann. Letters to Jerome Agel, Jan. 26 and March 5, 1976.

Wilhelmi, H. Ph. Letter to Jerome Agel, April 15, 1976.

Willard, Jo. Letters to Jerome Agel, March 23 and April 15, 1976.

Williams, Tennessee. *Memoirs.* New York: Doubleday, 1975.

Winakor, Bess. "The Most Restrictive Diet: Just Don't Eat—Anything." *Chicago Sun-Times,* Aug. 19, 1975: 33.

Women's Wear Daily. "At Shrubland Hall." March 14, 1975: 13.

———. "Faster, Faster." Feb. 13, 1976.

Wren, Christopher S. "Soviet Jew, Denied Exit, Continues Fast." *The New York Times,* April 21, 1975.

Yogananda, Paramahansa. "The Physical and Spiritual Rewards of Fasting." Self-Realization Fellowship, Los Angeles, Calif.

Youmans, John B. "Hunger and Malnutrition." Letter to the Editor, *Journal of the American Medical Association* 214 (6) 1970: 1123.

Young, V. R., et al. "Potential Use of 3-Methylhistidine Excretion as an Index of Progressive Reduction in Muscle Protein Catabolism during Starvation." *Metabolism: Clinical and Experimental* 22 (11) 1973: 1429–36.

———. "Protein Requirements of Man: Comparative Nitrogen Balance Response within the Submaintenance-to-maintenance Range of Intakes of Wheat and Beef Proteins." *Journal of Nutrition* 105 (5) 1975: 534–42.

In addition, there were innumerable interviews with and correspondence from patients of Dr. Cott.

ABOUT THE AUTHORS

ALLAN COTT, M.D., author of *Fasting: The Ultimate Diet,* is a psychiatrist in private practice in New York City and on the attending staff, Gracie Square Hospital, where he has fasted patients. He is a Life Fellow of the American Psychiatric Association, Founding Fellow and President of the Academy of Orthomolecular Psychiatry, Consultant to the Allan Cott School for children with severe disorders of behavior, communication, and learning, and Consultant to the Spear Educational Center for severely disturbed children. He is the author of many articles on the treatment of mental illness in adults and on the treatment of seriously disturbed children and learning disabled children with the use of vitamins, minerals and dietary control.

JEROME AGEL, co-author of *Fasting: The Ultimate Diet,* has been involved in seventeen major books as author, co-author, and/or producer. They include *22 Fires* (a novel); *The Cosmic Connection* and *Other Worlds* (with Carl Sagan); *Herman Kahnsciousness; The Making of Kubrick's 2001; The Medium is the Massage* (with Marshall McLuhan); *It's About Time & It's About Time* (with Alan Lakein; *Understanding Understanding* (with Humphry Osmond); and *I Seem To Be a Verb* (with Buckminster Fuller). He contributed on a regular basis to *The New York Times Magazine.*

EUGENE BOE, co-author of *Fasting: The Ultimate Diet,* has co-authored or contributed to fifteen books, including *The Immigrant Experience, Hart's Guide to New York City,* and *Cooking Creatively with Natural Foods.* He is the co-author of the novel *22 Fires.* His articles have appeared in numerous national magazines.

How's Your Health?

Bantam publishes a line of informative books, written by top experts to help you toward a healthier and happier life.

SPECIAL
MONEY SAVING
OFFER

Now you can have an up-to-date listing of Bantam's hundreds of titles plus take advantage of our unique and exciting bonus book offer. A special offer which gives you the opportunity to purchase a Bantam book for only 50¢. Here's how!

By ordering any five books at the regular price per order, you can also choose any other single book listed (up to a $4.95 value) for just 50¢. Some restrictions do apply, but for further details why not send for Bantam's listing of titles today!

Just send us your name and address plus 50¢ to defray the postage and handling costs.